The Science of Life

The rules of proper life

By

Bernard Benson Sarfo

The Science of Life

Bernard Benson Sarfo

Published by Bernard Benson Sarfo, 2024.

While every precaution has been taken in the preparation of this book, the publisher assumes no responsibility for errors or omissions, or for damages resulting from the use of the information contained herein.

THE SCIENCE OF LIFE

First edition. February 16, 2024.

ISBN: 979-8224291540

Written by Bernard Benson Sarfo.

Also by Bernard Benson Sarfo

The Fact Among Facts (1st)
The Fact Among Facts

Standalone
The Youth Murderer
Be Original Not a Copy
The Christians Science or Scholarship
Precious than Paradise
Habit makes future
A shelter from storm and rain
The Science of Life
The Strongest Lion Knockback
The Perfect and Inspiring City

Dedication

I dedicate this book to everyone in the world today and wish them courage!

Dedication

I dedicate this book to everyone in the world today and wish them courage!

'When wisdom entered into your heart, and knowledge is pleasant unto your soul, discretion shall preserve you, understanding shall keep you' (Proverbs 2:10, 11).

Introduction

This world is full of tragedies, dangers and damages. Life in this world cannot be entirely rosy, contrary to the expectation of human. There are lots of obstacles across all the things we do in the world.

Passing through the world is guided by natural laws, which we should observe. People of today want to live in the world without laws and do whatever pleases them. Life cannot be without laws.

Every human being in the world must be prepared to face the practical realities of life in the world – the opportunities, defeats, duties and successes.

Life, as we may be aware of, is not about arrogant; it includes preparation, planning, fortitude, activity, gentleness, integrity, pure thought, choice and readiness. Everything we do turns to us either for good or bad. Life is like a tree; it bears fruit. What you sow is what you reap.

Now the world is moving to the end, everything testifies. Two different voices are sounding and the voices have the identity that makes the difference of signal and resulted in life-and-death. Which one are you hearing? And what is your nature today?

The youth of today are taking life for granted. Harming themselves about life issues that are on call for and damaging their destiny in exchanging their life success for weeds reward. Many youths are digging holes for themselves because of their actions and wishes, and do not take advice but proud themselves in wickedness act.

Many negative actions are hoarding up among the youth causing their ruin without a cure. The youth must know how to build the true-life foundation at their early stage, and to take care of their acts. To know the best for their life and to know what life is it about.

The world has moved into calamities difficult to understand and hard to measure the result of sin in humans' life. People are crying day and night. Many are suffering within and without desperate for relief but there is no answer to their difficulties. And there are unseen agonies around the globe and people are anxious for liberty but who will care or ask and seek to help? All human beings need to look beyond the outward towards one another. Many are suffering under the covering but who will consider and help?

Human selfishness has become a wall to prevent one another to help the needy ones. Many people have lost the right direction and strife for a good position but there is no sign of hope, and they are shouting for help but there's no reaction.

There are famines of poverty beyond human control killing many people in the world today. And those who are rich pretend and close their eyes towards those who don't have and living out of service to their fellow.

This book is to remind us of the service we own to ourselves and to prompt us on the charity we must put into practice each day for everyone and do away wickedness act that goes on every day. Let us help one another because God created us to do so.

Further, No man no woman and no woman no man. The servant is the foundation for the master and the master is the protective wall for the servant. However, home maid is the key for the mistress and, the mistress is the room for the maid. When one is absent, it can affect the other. Then everyone needs help from the another, without that; the life will be difficult for each one of us. We all need help to survive.

This book also reminds us to know what to do to one another and what we must do to have the best of life, and to advise people to be watchful about the things they do because they will account for them (Gal 6:7).

We prosper in life when we recognize God in all our activities. Every human being in the world must be aware of this! Why buy what profits nothing? This book can change you and makes you up to the target of life!

Many people of today are selfish and they only think of their success and fame. Others have already succeeded and enjoyed themselves with only their friends and families and then leave others.

It is not surprising that those who are rich always content with their life but not others. Means that, some rich men do not regard the poor men through the wealth they have.

Many people are suffering from poverty and nothing to hope for. What extra do you think? What is your mind? How mindful are you to the people around you?

Are you willing to help others who are weak? It is your wish to help others? What do you seek for others in your community? Is it your concern that your community will develop to the first class in the world?

Are you ready to set an example for someone to know and learn from you? Africans always depend on their government to do for them. They always wait for the government to develop their community for them.

Do you want your own to flourish than others? What extra do you think? It is my wish that everyone will learn how to support and help his or her community development and then help others who are weak.

The purpose of this message is to let you know the reason of your being on the earth. Then to learn to support and encourage those who are weak and have lost hope in their life.

Do not only seek your good and welfare but seek the welfare of others and support them to succeed as you have succeeded. Do not be selfish but be selfless and help others like yourself.

God created the world for service and development. All things serve and depend on others to succeed. You cannot develop without someone's aid.

Why do you don't want to help others to succeed like you? You need to change your style of living and then support others and your community development.

Contents pages

1. What makes you different?

It is not all the birds that sing the sweet song but there is a bird which sings a song for moves or dancing. What do I mean? There is something that makes differences between people.

We all have identities and characters. Here, everyone must come out with something that makes his or her name. It is difficult to identify a person without his or her activities. But the difference comes from acts or behaviour.

It is not your words that makes the difference but your actions. Your words are your witness but your action is your security. In fact, you cannot be famous unless you act accordingly.

It is not just a word but the behaviour. What is your goal? Where do you focus? What do you want to do? Many people have failed because of selfishness. Others have been broken because of greedy.

What have you planned to do? Life is how you want it but fame is an art of action you have made. You need to do something that supersedes what others have done. The difference is the name you will get at the end. Do you cheat others by your power? What makes you different? Each one of us must have something unique that identifies his or her personality.

Actions and words of a person make his or her character. But attitude answers the results. In fact, our life on this earth has shortened and it is not God's wish at the beginning.

But whatever your life, it must impact on people for good. That is, you must do something exceptional for recognition. What have you done for your recognition?

It is not your wealth that makes you exceptional but your attitude. There are many things that form our attitude; dresses, speech, walk and the others.

All these make a person and the identity of each individual. What character are you forming? Whatever you do, forms your identity or character.

There are a lot for us to do as human beings. Everyone must do something that will serve as an example for others to benefit from it. It is not what you do but what you do from the love that matters. We always sometimes want to do things that will let others know our fame but does not do things that will let others recognize our goodness.

Your greatness does not come by your words but it comes by your act of love that makes another benefit. So, it is time for you to do something that will make you a good name forever.

You must speak differently; see differently, dress differently, sing differently, eat differently and then act differently. But it must impact for good but not for evil.

You must be different altogether from all people; in your actions, in your dress, in speech and your walk. In fact, your life must be different from others. You must live differently from others.

You must have different faith and character. You must be exceptional from others. You must see differently from whatever others see. Be unique and prudent in all matters of life. You need to do something that will make you different altogether.

You must leave a legacy to your children's children. You haven't done anything yet. You must do something and then make a good account of your life.

You should not depend on the opinions of others to live your life, but you must decide for yourself and live uniquely. You must learn and teach at the same time, but you must be unlike others.

You must do things appropriate than the others. Make difference between right and wrong; clean and unclean. You must show dignity and knowledge in all your doings.

Try to do things well and then makes a difference in your appearance. You must welcome others with good approach and decency. Let the world consider your legacy and your fame that have a good name and glorify God about it.

What makes you different? Have you done something that others will benefit from it? In all, do the right thing and then let others learn from it. They all looking at you, what are you leaving for them?

2. What extra do you think?

In all, life consists of all-round education and the character by which nothing can be compared. It is not as you think that makes you dear, but it is by your words and actions that testifies you.

Life is not about self-esteem but dignity and honesty. You must not think that you have done what you can without faithfulness. Means you must do above the ability which you think is enough.

That is, you must do more than expected for recognition. Whatever you do must be on its way and it must be recognized for future reference. Your life must be fruit for someone and cloth that clothes naked.

You must go beyond what you have imagined. That is, you must help others by the way you can and above. It is not enough to help others with their needs.

Always keep on helping, do not stop but continue as you eat every day. In fact, life is not about you, but it is for others aid which builds yours well. Do not be selfish but be selfless and then know how to help others. What do I want you to learn from this content which is the title of this book? Many people think that life is all about self, but it is not so. It is about sacrificing for others.

There are a lot to do in life and a lot to share. You cannot be your own but you must be for others. Means share and continue sharing until you die. What extra do you think?

Means you should not be selfish on whatever you know or do, but let others benefit from you're doing. Also, means do not hoard up for your benefit, but let others enjoy your belongings.

If someone fills up with goods and other things, that person does not mind anything again. He or she does not care for the others, whether it will be well with or not.

The person enjoys only by his or herself families and then regardless of others. Everyone needs your help or support to make theirs complete. You should not be narrow-minded but think broadly and take note of others. Let others welfare be in your mind and then support them to succeed like you. You must think extra not for yourself but others benefit or wellbeing. Leave a legacy and let others learn from you.

Let others point you on your good works and then enjoy through your assistance. Be their song; their food and their dress. Be kind and always seek for the weak and then help them.

You must think beyond yourself and help others like yourself. Let your comfort be the others comfort and your joy others joy. Learn to forgive and welcome others with joy and appreciation.

Let them feel good and welcome at your presence. Be open to all people and wish them well. Do not be selfish but share and keep on sharing. Do not cease to do others well; whether they are enemies or not, help them when they need your help or not. Life is not for only self-benefiting but for all who need help.

You must think extra but not only for yourself but for others. In fact, you need to take note of others, not to discourage or laughing at, but to help as you can. Consider bad times whiles enjoying good times. That is, think extra about your doings and then consider the outcome. Do not be too good and do not be too bad, why are you challenging?

Let others shout their mouth on you and be at peace. It is not all but it must be something. Means keep yourself from questions and answer on the issues of certain matters. Means be exceptional and keep yourself well from suspicions. Give and let others take note of you for a good report. Spread your case and let others discuss.

Means let others mention your name with a good report and then prolong your life. Do away envy; selfishness, malice and greedy. Maintain your dignity and build your honest with enthusiasm and knowledge. Do good to all people and then maintain your good name.

You cannot have it easy but you shall overcome by faithfulness. Let others have fun with your little as well as big. Be food and money for others and then exchange your wreck for eternity. Do not enjoy with your own but let others enjoy with you. What extra do you think? You must be a help for others but not for yourself alone.

3. What can someone learn from you?

It does not matter your age, someone can learn from you. What have you done and then wanted to do more? Our life must serve as an example for others.

It is not big or the small you will do that determines your ability, but it depends on the honesty you will show on your daily activities that qualify your ability. Means, be honest in your work and do the best thing for a good reward.

You must be unique in all your doings. Do not let others question your work and ability of your doings. You can do more on how you have imagined and it can be better than what you have proposed.

Try and do the best of all the time concerning the work you have done previously. Let others ask of your ability and honest work. Avoid laziness in your work but do not work to abuse your ability.

Honour your health and regards the rules of health. Do not abuse yourself through hard work but work sufficiently. You need to be a mirror for others. That is, let others find their fault through your act or performance and then correct themselves. Be honest and do honest work.

Be an example and let others learn from you. Many people have failed to be an example of good works. But you need to be an exceptional, no matter the condition.

Tell the truth and eschew evil. Let others accuse and condemn you about your faithfulness but do not mind them. Stand for the truth and die in it. Consider your actions and makes a difference in comparison.

It is not good to pretend but work from the heart and challenge the truth. Means let others clap for you through honest work and self-denial. Do not bribe, yet do not cheat. Consider the little and know how to deal with the poor.

Do not answer anyone with anger but let your words witness your meekness. What have you done that will let others recognize you? Are you rough? Are you serious? Do you mind to do good to others? Are you ready to help the weak? In fact, my concern is to let you know what you can be to others through the little you know and can do for others aid. You can do something that will let others glorify God through you.

Be a blessing and let others bless you and bless themselves. Are you meek? Do you love others as yourself? What have you consider or thought of concerning your brother?

Oh, my dear, the world needs you to do something for them. Have you considered yourself well? Do you know you can do marvelous things? In fact, you can do something that no one can do.

You need to take note of yourself and then build yourself well in all matters of life. Be a servant to all men and serve God from the heart; mind and your strength.

Do not be wise at your estimation but learn every day from others. But consider little things and cherish positive mind. You need to do something and then let others recognize you.

Be industrious and honest as well. Be forceful and gentle as well. Let others take notes of you and then learn from you. What have you done to be recognized by others? Someone is watching to see something different and good from you. What will you do to be imitated by someone?

What I have seen that when African man builds a house and rent a store and then buy a car that is okay for him. He does not think further again concerning other matter which will benefit others and his community and the entire world.

This is not life and it cannot be a life. Selfish life is a dead life and it cannot be counted as life. Life is a service to mankind but not self-caring. You cannot make a life without serving others.

What everyone needs to ask is that, what have I done to my fellow beings or brothers and sisters? You must do something that others will be mentioning your name with.

Do not be selfish but be selfless and share whatever you have for others. Do the best of your time and use of every minute for the aid of others.

Let others know you by your service and honest. Do not do things only for your interest but the interest of others. What will others learn from you? Is it good or bad?

4. What is your idea?

What have you planned for and what do you want to do to help others? What difference do you want to make? What impact will you want to make? What is different about you? You need to plan and then set a target for your life.

Do not fail to plan; else you will plan to fail. Have a purpose or goals. Do not live without purpose; else you will be lazy and will not do anything for profit life.

You need to set something before you and then work towards it. Learn something and do something; else you will be miserable in life. If you did not plan to do something, you will not prosper.

What have you plan for? What do you want to do? In fact, if you do not have an aim, you will be there without doing anything and you cannot be anything as well. Life without a goal, is life without progress and lifeless.

You cannot be anyone unless you wish to be somebody. That is. Do not be aimless in life but set something before you and work towards it. Your knowledge is your life and your life is your knowledge. Correct attitude build correct life and wellbeing. But shortcut waste time and energy for nothing. In fact, inadequate knowledge brings inadequate income and fear of wants. But true knowledge brings sufficient income and the beautiful ends.

Your idea must base on creativity and innovation. Means you must do something that is important to the lives of others and yourself as well. You should sit there doing nothing, yet you will be useless in life.

But you must be prudent and then work with your hands for future expectation. You must impress people with action and knowledge. Do not earn your income by somebody's knowledge, if it is possible, try to set up something that will earn you income and then set yourself free from slavery in earning income. That is, use your talent to earn income that will serve you right. Do not be a waiter in life but be a producer and the director as well. You must think and use your time as well. You must be productive and distributer as well. Do not set your mind on one thing, but think broadly and set your goals well. You shall not bag but you shall lend to others by making the time dear. You must know yourself and know what you can do. Use your mind and then build the broken wall of your life. You must learn to the peak ends and set yourself free from all shortcomings.

Try to do something different in comparison to all innovations in the world. Do not go fast but go with the time and then avoid all mistakes in your journey. Means, do things right and then avoid shadow works.

Be forceful and prudent in all your doings. Be a hundred per cent worker and avoid inadequate work. Do not be specific time worker but work tirelessly but do not abuse yourself with too much work. Means work sufficiently and accurately. What do I want you to learn? You must use your mind and share what you have. Do not waste your time for not doing anything. But make use of the time and set yourself free. What is your idea? Means, what can you do to help others; your community and yourself? You must something that you will be remembered by the world.

5. Are you selfish?

What are you doing and what do you want to do for others? Self is the personality of a being or the state by which a person looks like. Your appearance witnesses your state but your act makes you self-centred or not.

In fact, whatever you do makes a position for you and it determines your state of being. What makes you selfish or self-centred? Everyone in the world has such kind of behave which makes his or her different from the other.

In all, everyone needs to shut this kind of attitude that cease the blessing that he or she must obtain. Selfishness makes someone greedy and unwelcome.

This kind of character makes a person fruitless and unproductive. It does away love, kindness and beauty of a person. Selfishness does not know anyone but only self. It prevents meekness and mercy.

It does not know grace and compassion. We all have something that makes us selfish. In fact, this kind of behaviour cannot be known by many of us, unless you that person have a position. It can take you captive and make a slave of sin. It does not matter your maturity and experience in life, you can be selfish.

What can this shortcoming lead you to? It can destroy your beauty of character and then disgrace you. Anyone selfish lacks love and mercy.

This act or behaviour avoids the spirit of God. Selfishness leads to fruitless and unproductive. Everyone needs to consider things well and then avoid greediness.

Do not entertain self but entertain selflessly. Let others know you by your charity. You need to consider others well and help the weak. Be mindful and alert to help.

Let others seek you with your act of charity. Do away grasping but share your belongings. Be plain and love others as yourself. Never discriminate but be free with all people.

Yet, be vigilant and accept all situations. Do not be as wicked by your act but be kind and share whatever you have to others. Do away selfishness and let others enjoy your possessions. You must know yourself well and then learn to correct your mistakes. In fact, this kind of fault disgrace people and close the doors of blessing.

Those who do not want to give or share with others cannot be prospered. We all have this fault and it needs to be corrected. Note; it is only the Spirit of God who can correct kind of fault for us.

Else we shall fail by our effort. What can you do to improve your ability in giving? What have you planned to make someone dear with the little you have? I want you to do something for your brothers and sisters around you. Do not be selfish but be liberal for all people at your society. Let them praise you through giving.

Always consider yourself and consider people not to hurt them by your wrong act. But learn to give always and be ready to support the weak and everyone who needs your help. Do not hoard up but share and then receive a blessing. What will be your benefit, if you have the whole world and then lose your life? Give and continue in giving and then receive the blessing with no comparison.

6. The beauty of character

Oh! What a beautiful character? There many people who are always ready to help and rescue. They always wish others well and welcome them. What have you done that witness your character as beautiful?

These people always seek to help the needed ones. They love beauty and love charity. It is their attitude and behaviour. They have allowed God to lead them constantly and can't be satisfied unless they share what they have.

It is their wish and joy to give constantly. They love liberal and cherish sharing. They have prepared themselves and are ready to support. These people do not wait for others to ask from them, but they seek and help as well.

Have you done this before? All the creatures serve and support as well. If you do not want to serve, then you refuse to want to live. Anyone who does not want to share or serve, do not want to live.

You need to share or serve and then live. Blessings come by giving and sharing the little you have. In all, everyone must take note that the little donation makes abundant of blessings in which we do not know. Those who engage in it preserve their lives and their future children. You must learn to serve and give as well. Do not be afraid to share important information or knowledge. Do your best, to tell the truth; do not be afraid to tell it vividly.

But be considerate not to fail of doing well to others. Else, your truth-telling will be questionable. Go on and share; do not be hesitate to tell truth and make your words comfort and purely.

Be light for others and food as well. That is, let people know you by your good advice and giving. Share your cloth and sandals with others. Means give without considering yourself first.

But let others enjoy first and wait for yours later. Do not take note when you are sharing, but share without consideration. Means do not discriminate or partial in sharing. Everyone needs your help, do not withhold from them. There are more to do for others and it needs patience and sympathy to do that. You cannot do away the other or one, but you need to do all for the benefit of others. Good speech revives the soul and then gives peace to the listener. But poor speech disturbs the spirit and then discourages audience.

Wise people love beauty and decency. Those who love liberality love others and then love the openness. This character makes life dear and cheerful. You need to note that, those who love the beauty of character love giving and rescue the souls from burdens.

What character are you building? Will you mind to help others? Do not be greedy but share and set others free from poverty slavery. Beautiful character builds and repairs the brokenhearted.

It loves to give and love to welcome others. My concern is to let you know the benefit of giving and sharing. There is nothing profitable and blessing than giving and sharing. The beauty is that you can become a friend to all people and beloved to all age group. Set yourself as a giver or donor to all people and then become all-time people friend. It will lead you to uncalculated blessings to you and future generation

7. Be honest and devotee

Let nothing discourage you, be bold and strong in all stages. Life is not easy but you can achieve your goal if you determine it. There are a lot of discourages and disturbances all over the globe.

But there is something that everyone should know concern life and its best gain. You cannot, dare, do away. If you dare, you cannot prosper no matter what you will do.

You cannot get it whole if you avoid these keys I am about to let you know. Note: pure life consists of these two things honest and commitment. These two are the keys of pure life and the best of gain or profit.

In fact, honest life is a profitable life than any life that man has live. But honesty without devotion makes less profit. You cannot develop or profit without one of these two.

You need these two things and then to make your life complete. You need to be honest and ardent to achieve the greatness of life. Life cannot be life without these two; honesty and devotion. In fact, whatever man can do; depends on sacrifice to make it done. Else, it will end nothing. Our whole life consists of these acts to earn a profit. Without devotion and honesty; the life of a man will be lifeless.

You need to be honest and a devotee at the same time, else you will not achieve the total sum of life. Be honest and supportive as well. That is, help people to succeed or achieve their goal through faithfulness and welfare.

Do not hesitate to help the weak and the poor. Do honest work and then support others to succeed. You must work hard and do away laziness. Do not deceive yourself or others but be honest in all your doings.

You must help everyone when you are needed. Do not confuse people by a false message. But let your words flow with honey and milk. That is, be honest of your speech and then others respect you.

Be watchful and build yourself well for good works. Do not cheat to gain wealth. Yet do honest work and then achieve your wealth. Devote yourself to others welfare and then prevent envy. Consider everyone and know how to live with others. Think extra for the aid of others. Try to build hope for the hopeless and then rescue perishing and care for the dying. Support others on the way you can and let them know you love them.

It is not late to start life afresh at any age when you think you are late. Means, there is hopeful at any stage in life even when you are old enough as you cannot do anything again. Honest build life even when things are falling apart.

Devote your time and energy for people and serve today and then save your life in future. Do not fold your hands and wait for others to do for you, but do by yourself and for others and then prevent speechlessly.

You need to have your blessing by effort and doings. Only be honest and devotee for others. Maintain your dignity and forcefulness. Do not be too gentle that prevent socialization. But consider every condition and then know how to cope with for the aid of others and sake. Be authentic and devotee for others and then build your future hope as well. What extra do you think?

8. Be knowledgeable and intelligent

What have you supposed? What have you considered? Do not be as anyone but be someone who knows his or her duty and service. Consider your move and acts. Know how to associate with others and support them.

To do this well, you need to have knowledge and enthusiasm. In all, you must be intelligent or smart to do it perfectly. As human beings, we are ungrateful and sinful as well.

It is difficult to deal with men when you do not have a patient. Our ways of life are tricks and wickedness by nature. We all love beauty but fail to do what is right and true.

Everyone wants his or her glory than the glory of others. Do not do something will cause your brother to stumble. Be careful always when you are dealing with your brother or sister.

Means do not show any act contrary to the principles of to your brother or sister. That is, do not show negative appearance to anyone whether poor or rich; big or small, short or tall. Try your best to associate well with all people. Be social but not as a fool, be intelligent but not as a thief, be prudent but as a cheater. You need the knowledge to build your house and then need the knowledge to do things well. Means that, without knowledge, you cannot do things properly.

It will be difficult for you to do things a reasonable way when lacks knowledge. In all your doings get knowledge and wisdom. You must educate yourself well, and be quick at the same. That is, use your mind or think and then solve problems of the others.

Do not wait to solve problems for others and do not let somebody prompt you on the things you can do for others. Else you did not act wisely or intelligently. Be alert to help and solve problems for your brothers or sisters who are weak.

Somebody needs your help and you must seek and help the needy. In all, act intelligently when you are helping others. That is, do not show partiality in supporting others about their needs.

You need to think extra in whatever you are doing. Consider the big and small equally in assisting them. Be careful not to throw dust in anyone's eyes. That is, ceased to looking to others face continuously and then prevent cheating in your sharing. That is, do away partiality when you are giving to many people at the same place.

Life consists of smartness; knowledge, honesty and self-control. These are the keys that built proper life in the sight of man. You need to keep these things and then know how to live with all men.

If you lack one of these keys, you will not complete life as its demand. That is, why it takes time for one to achieve good wealth. The wealth that is achieved by cheating does not last. But the wealth that is achieved by patience and truth last.

Do not take things for granted but note every act or deeds that you preceded. You need to take note of every action you intend. You must do things above ignorance and then prove your knowledge and intelligence.

Do not boast when you do right but consider the outcome and stay cool. In all, remember your Creator and keep on doing your part as can to people who needs your help. Do not repent when you share something important to your brother or sister. Shout your mouth when you help someone.

Do not disclose to other person concerning what you have done to someone. But let it be in secret and then receive your best reward from your Father in Heaven.

Do things right and also prevent discourage in your speech. You must cherish and seek knowledge and then apply it in your doings. Let it be your song; your food and shelter. It shall build you and prepare you for the future. Knowledge will save you and others from poverty.

It will guide you from mistaking and keep you on track. Be smart and knowledgeable with enthusiasm and honesty. What extra do you think? As this book title is letting you act intelligently, and then prompt you to do away selfishness from your life. Will you mind?

9. The Boys acts

Actions are the signs of every person identity and the nature of that being. Somebody's attitude is known by the actions been revealed, and the result testifies the personality of that character. Naturally, human beings are known for their actions and the nature of that action witness the foundation set up.

The world has lessons which must be considering. What we must not be forgotten is the death penalty that everyone must face. Life is the fruit that one's needs to be bear.

That is, life needs considerations and the way it must go. Many have failed because of the lack of guidance and have missed the target because of the wrong attitude. If there is vanity of life ever live in the world, is the life of the youth.

The youthful age is the age of miss conceptions of life uncertain to decide the result, but acts of every youth can set up the period of good or bad future. The youthful age acts have about 85 per cent of good or bad life ever lived. That is, the life destiny is set at that stage or time, and all the future result rest on that era which many of the youth, do not have any knowledge about it and behave indecently.

Many youths joke and do whatever they like and never mind any advice giving to them when they feel their mature to do for themselves. In fact, inexperienced life results in mismanagement and even damage the laws that govern life matters; Means life without guide behave like sea waves without a purpose of ambition that makes life proper stopover.

In life, youth have a lot to play than the elderly; means that, their chance in life matters are best and bigger to have what it takes about life goal. But many of the youth neglect their ability to have good results.

Many boys take life for granted and behave whichever they wish. Roughing act has become their food every day. Disrespect attitude is shown every moment.

Boys, you can run before dog but not the wild lion, means you can do whatever you like at your stage today, but you cannot escape the bad day ahead. Never joke about your time today, whiles you have the strength to do whatever you wish. Today is yours but tomorrow can be your worse ever had. Hello! Boy, is there anything you need to consider about life today? Or is there any lesson you must study today about tomorrow's life? Sure! You can't predict the beauty of your future life, but you can know the result of today's acts toward tomorrow.

Besides, today's acts are evidence of future fruit. And the actions of the body are the laws that govern the body, whether bad or good witness the start point of that life. Whichever act we allow have what its produce and that act product can result in unforgotten mark throughout the life last and that is to be considered about today's acts.

Never as youth joke about today's life and do whatever you like. Life is not like swimming in the fresh pool under trees a hot day. Life is not smooth like cotton made up of a dress. But life is hard like digging rocky field without using the proper tool for the digging.

Means you cannot have what you need easy unless you come across somebody's treasure. That is, leftover possessions but without correct experienced about life matters; you cannot manage it well that, which concerns the rules of life best live. Boys out there must be vigilant about today's acts and be able to harvest correct fruit in the future.

Note what the Bible says;

Eccl.11: 9, 10

You who are young, be happy while you are young, and let your heart give you joy in the days of your youth. Follow the ways of your heart and whatever your eyes see, but know that for all these things God will bring you into judgment.

So then, banish anxiety from your heart and cast off the troubles of your body, for youth and vigour are meaningless.

Life is a choice and wish, you can live by your will no one will question you. But know that, you are going to reap what you sow and bear any result. And note that once again, life has one chance and there is no other life in today's world which you can try again. Means the only opportunity you have is living as a being today, there is no other second chance of life when you lose it today. The only left for you is judgment and the reward of your choice. Consider this scripture;

Eccl.12:1-7

Remember your Creator in the days of your youth, before the days of trouble come and the years approach when you will say, "I find no pleasure in them"—

2 before the sun and the light and the moon and the stars grow dark, and the clouds return after the rain;

3 when the keepers of the house tremble, and the strong men stoop, when the grinders cease because they are few, and those looking through the windows grow dim;

4 when the doors to the street are closed and the sound of grinding fades; when people rise up at the sound of birds, but all their songs grow faint;

5 when people are afraid of heights and of dangers in the streets; when the almond tree blossoms and the grasshopper drags itself along and desire no longer is stirred. Then people go to their eternal home and mourners go about the streets.

6 Remember him—before the silver cord is severed, and the golden bowl is broken; before the pitcher is shattered at the spring, and the

wheel broken at the well, 7 and the dust returns to the ground it came from, and the spirit returns to God who gave it.

.Note;

Never acts as if there is no judgment or the reward of any act. Remember that every life ever live has a reward and there is no way of escape.

Put off clumpy acts and respect life laws, make a prudent decision for better live acts and discover what is best for your life reward. You can enjoy life but consider the act about it. Every Youth must run out before fornication and be alert for life issues.

The youth must stop indiscipline behaviour and act decency that calls for a good name and stops embarrassment acts. Life never favours and does not respect anyone who wants to survive and have the best condition ever. But when care is taking, there is abundant joy. There is no other day than today and there is no other occasion than you have today. The opportunity days are days off that you exist and there is no other hour than the hour you exist, improve your being and do the most of every hour you find yourself in.

what are your concerns? What are you focusing on? What do you suggest? What is your purpose? What do you love to do? And what actions are you want to make?

Youthful age is very important and if there is anytime best in human's life, is the youthful stage. I call it the age of the sound body and correct mind hour and the best choice stage. But the youth do not mind the result of their acts concerns their life then and fail in the life purpose.

The youth need to seek knowledge and wisdom at that hour of their life. And make every effort to improve their life journey. They must listen to their parents and pay attention to instructions. Life is not a joke but fate.

Let's consider this scripture;

Proverb 2:1-12

My son, if you accept my words and store up my commands within you,2 turning your ear to wisdom and applying your heart to understanding—

3 indeed, if you call out for insight and cry aloud for understanding,4 and if you look for it as for silver and search for it as for hidden treasure,5 then you will understand the fear of the Lord and find the knowledge of God.

6 For the Lord gives wisdom; from his mouth come knowledge and understanding.7 He holds success in store for the upright, he is a shield to those whose walk is blameless,

8 for he guards the course of the just and protects the way of his faithful ones. 9 Then you will understand what is right and just and fair—every good path.

10 For wisdom will enter your heart, and knowledge will be pleasant to your soul.11 Discretion will protect you, and understanding will guard you.

12 Wisdom will save you from the ways of wicked men, from men whose words are perverse,

The youth must be very considerate at their stage and do their business as their age-mate; means their stage is very favourable and they must be aware and do brilliant things.

Boys, as we called, must take life serious and count the cost of every performance at their stage. And note that, they will reap the sowed seed fruit. The world is large but your actions can be larger than it.

That is, your actions can bring a countless result that you cannot margin and destroy as many as the blessings can count and you cannot cancel the mark of that identity caused.

One mistake can destroy thousands of blessings and make life worse for you. I am saying this from experienced and the lessons that I have been through in life.

Never live as you wish or move as the flesh wish but fear God and honour him in all your doings and live according to the life principles.

Youth must take advice and live a worthy life. What will be the result of regardless of instruction?

Note: what the bible is saying;

Proverb 13:18 says; whoever disregards discipline comes to poverty and shame, but whoever heeds correction is honoured.

The youth, must consider their acts and take care of life. Whichever act we intend resulted in good or bad for life. Let's watch out and set up a moral example and make the right decision.

Proverb13:10

Where there is strife, there is pride, but wisdom is found in those who take advice.

The youth must manage their life well and think. Choose what will make your life beautiful at the end and manage every situation and decide what is best and worthy for your life.

Note Psalms 119:9-11

9 How can a young person stay on the path of purity? By living according to your word.

10 I seek you with all my heart; do not let me stray from your commands.

11 I have hidden your word in my heart,

that I might not sin against you.

This must be your joy and interest and take note of your steps and be a blessing!

10. The Women proud acts

The worse of life ever practice and the most disadvantage behaviour that causes the doom of life; thinks of self-beauty or being proud of one's self in the manner of self-important or agreeable yourself than the other. These acts revolve on ladies (women).

The practice of competition among women is higher than men. And the manner, in which it is practice, has caused damage to all people in the world. Women weakness has damaged the world beauty in terms of correct life management. Women always feel proud and wish the acts of flesh than the spiritual.

The girls have picked these acts and want to live by sentiment. There is nothing so dangerous than to feel proud of yourself and behave by your emotion. Girls sometimes act as if they are on top of everyone.

Ladies who enter university level, some regardless of their colleagues who haven't. Some women feel proud of their beauty and want to take advantage of everything concerns life.

Today's young girls have taken the illegal track and attitude contrary to life principles and are doing what they like. They have taken their shoulders up and behave like birds fighting on food.

That is, they are always ready to promote evil acts and ready to stand for their right to do that. Girls always want to challenge themselves and act as if no one is like them; they feel pompous and want to show off.

You cannot stand well whiles you are on the muddy area. That is, you can't have a good atmosphere by your negative attitude and you cannot push without position yourself well.

Means every act in life comes by intent and the result makes the difference. They must be honest and prudent to have a remarkable name and praiseworthy; which is valuable and admire by people.

In fact, life is not in fashion. But it is principles and the fate matter. Young ladies must have patient about life and move wisely. They are to take note of every step they make and fixed their steps well. Girls must be alert about their life and manage it well. All acts have what it takes about life and nothing can be done well without good attention. Your misused life today is the penalty at your future scandal.

Never abuse your life by sexual immorality or other things else and lose your wealth. You can lose your gold because of your acts and dismantle your life diamond hardly to repair or refine as you wish at first.

That is, you cannot have your quality life again if you lose it. You must consider everything you do and beware of the shoes you ware. That is, be careful about in and out actions and manners. You must build your life with a good attitude and special ingredients for your beautiful praise.

Proverb 14:1-4

Says;

The wise woman builds her house, but with her own hands the foolish one tears hers down.

2 Whoever fears the Lord walks uprightly, but those who despise him are devious in their ways.

3 A fool's mouth lashes out with pride, but the lips of the wise protect them.

4 Where there are no oxen, the manger is empty, but from the strength of an ox come abundant harvests.

The effort introduces in everything, erect good or bad fruit but carefulness in doing brings the welcome atmosphere and results in peace life. If you want yourself good, good will come, equally the bad ends the same.

Young women must be careful about in and out actions and make a prudent decision for themselves and never lose the opportunity they have, else they will go through tremors they will never forget.

They must live carefully and watch their acts towards everything they do. Life is not like quiet sleep or resting in the guest house, but it is a continuous fight, that needs not rest or stop. One mistake causes much trouble and destroys life ability and brings life penalties.

Currently, ladies have made the world so dirty and have destroyed correct thinking because of their attitude in dress, and they never mind the consequence. In fact, the world today is for the women and the women are for the world! Everything in the world is now moving by the women and the world has damage through the manner of their appearance. This is true and there is no doubt about it and many of them witness and even make comments on that. It is their news and it bears evidence against them!

If adult women will change their style of living and make a good example as prudent women, the young girls will make the world beauty as rosy and the world will take its healthy cloth again. Following the world beauty is nothing but the fear of God makes a difference.

Note this scripture;

Proverbs 31:30, 31

Charm is deceptive, and beauty is fleeting; but a woman who fears the Lord is to be praised.31 Honor her for all that her hands have done, and let her works bring her praise at the city gate.

The acts shown today by many young girls are horrible and it needs attention. How some of them behave is unacceptable. When life takes bad root it goes beyond the margin, and it is difficult to dig for the end. But many of them entertain it.

In fact, women are far advance in negative attitudes than men and it is obvious. They know how to hide sin than digging or searching for gold. Obviously, women can control the men by their acts and dismantle the good name ever known.

If the women take off their negative hat, the sun of rain will forever cease and the world we live today will be light of happiness. What am

I want to say; the world we live today can be fair and the best place to stay depends on the style of the women willing to live.

The attitude of many young girls has deformed many of the boys today. In fact, when it comes to the character as we all knew that makes a person. Many women do not care about their acts or never mind to show the negative side of it, to disturb their colleagues and are ready even to do more to make it worse. This is true, they mean to sin than to spare.

Further, women are pretenders or want to show off or pretend to be good-looking. Women are very pretenders and have deceived acts than men. Many women acts are deceptions and always want to defend their false acts.

The world we live in has a lot of lessons and notes to be considered. This world cannot cover it beauty again till Christ comes and there is no other chance that can be entertaining for the best life.

But if care is taking, we will benefit some positive lifestyle. The only thing we can do is to be careful about the way we live and take note about every step we make. The Lord is coming!

Many acts are destroying our being every day and night that result in eternal death but the women always entertain it. In fact, if women will decide to live a positive life, this world will somehow turn a bit positive atmosphere and the storms that always take men will semi-cease. However, life lessons are notes to correct the wrong acts but if we neglect the experience that resulted, then, we cannot cover it again as we wish. Misuse life has nothing to cover again in the best state as a wish but the life well managed can have what it takes.

Many girls put their life into a second fiddle and wish to act fleshly. They think that everything is normal and considered not. Eating as they wish and walk as they like; cloth anyhow and never listen to the advice or take note of the life matters.

Women can change the world; if they consider the life principles and live according to the laws govern the lives acts, then nothing will be needed again for best life traffic.

If the women will manage life according to its best and take care of their acts, then men will cease from mind murdering and have their being as a whole. Women must consider their acts and live modestly.

Note this scripture:

1Peter 3:1-5

Wives, in the same way, submit yourselves to your own husbands so that, if any of them do not believe the word, they may be won over without words by the behavior of their wives, 2 when they see the purity and reverence of your lives.

3 Your beauty should not come from outward adornment, such as elaborate hairstyles and the wearing of gold jewelry or fine clothes.

4 Rather, it should be that of your inner self, the unfading beauty of a gentle and quiet spirit, which is of great worth in God's sight.

5 For this is the way the holy women of the past who put their hope in God used to adorn themselves. They submitted themselves to their own husbands.

There is nothing short in nature, which needs to be modified or refine in another way for the best use. The things created were perfect from the beginning and well, please.

But suddenly something strange happened and things created to lose the exact state of its nature. Every act affects and can be resulted negatively or positively at the end. One mistake can create damage without remedy and can earn in eternal lose.

Women must be carefully considering their actions in any manner of life and they must watch out their dress-wearing currently. The miserable state of the world today stands on the manner of the women clothes themselves and the stylish of it nature appear in public causing mind disease and blocking correct nature of thinking, increasing lust of the eye and resulted in shamefulness.

There is nothing so dangerous than making yourself stumbling block for others or plan to make people fall by your appearance by pretending.

At the moment, women purposely appear in the manner that causes mental or spiritual fall, to destroy correct thinking and to set trap for people to lose their life.

Women today have totally decided their stand in dressing and shown the side which they are and decide their eternal home by the manner of their cloth; never put me wrong, I am telling you the truth.

Every dress wear represents the character and the manner of your appearance shows what you have decided. Many people do not know what they are about in life and what they are doing about life, taking things for granted and behaving as they wish.

Most of the women are so serious to act negatively and never mind to create what will cause harm to other people's lives and many of them are happy in doing that.

Your act can decide your destiny and can make a negative or positive home for you. All things done on earth have the peak or low estimate which can complete or incomplete of the project of life been set up.

Women love eyes beauty than inner beauty and promote weeds than the seed. That is, they loved what will destroy a few days than what will last long or wish moment than hours or days.

They love food ready to eat, than the food preparing to eat, that is, they want things fast than waiting before the best time and that is their lot that is why we are all suffering today. Women are the keys and the men are the doors, women can lock and open men in all matters of life and men have no say. Women have access to life avenues, and they are welcome everywhere in the world because they have the key of access; but they never know because of lack of self-actualization and they lack considering about life issues.

They weigh all things light and considered not the outcome. Women lack the spirit of forgiveness and they are also ready to curse than to bless when they are offended.

They lack patience in life but ready to provoke than to make happiness. Many of them are very lazy and not willing to work from the heart. They are gossip and active in making fun of others and to pull down others dignity.

All these acts deform their beauty and closed their insight for earning the best life at the end. Many of them lack understanding and difficult to accept their fault. But women have control, because of their attractive form.

And if care is taking, they can turn the world around in its better state and the world will be partially nice. As the strong wind sometimes throw out dust to the eyes of the people, so to the women who intentionally dress negatively makes dust around the globe for to hurt many eyes and to destroy the correct thinking with their acts.

Women must take care of how they act in all manners of life. I wonder why women love the world and its goods that benefit nothing and always hoard up belongings.

In fact, this world cannot and will not give anything worthy and help otherwise. But if women will be vigilant and decide what is right about life, then the world will shire and favour all of us and life will be fair. This message needs your consideration!

11. The unthinkable age acts

The world has a lot of notes and many incidents difficult to understand. Things are going on marvellously in the sight of man today seriously aggressive in the things ever happen before.

Young boys and girls are very vanity at their stage in terms of acts that always going on their life. Their age has no competition in life and because of their dependency; most of them don't think about what will happen tomorrow.

They live as they wish without attention. But life results depend on this stage whether good or bad. If there are stages in life which must be carefully considered; it is the young stage.

Children must be taught and train as well and monitored all the time. Their stage needs much attention from their parents and considers their act at each moment.

The children do not consider life matters but act from pressure and wish. They need to be directed by their parents every time. Many parents fail on how they should monitor their children but they only think about what they will eat and dress and leave the rest that matters. That is, their conducts are out of counting by their parents but this shouldn't be.

The basic acts of children are the penalty of their future goal and the harvest is managed by the grounds promoted or sowed. They should behave well and think of the result.

Children are like stream form by the raining water that does not have direction and can be lost at each time the rain ceased. That is, they do not have any stand when it comes to life as it should be live.

They need support and guide to survive by their parents. Correct Life management starts with the correct management in the childhood stage by their parents' guide and the fruit that bears depends on the act managed at their stage by their parents.

Children must be caring seriously by their parents and support as well. In fact, life results mostly stand on the acts in the childhood stage and as the results of this, parents must be very close to their children at the age of three to ten years. This age holds the deeper form of acts resulted in good or bad in the future of their children. Children do not think but behave to show their thinking.

That is why the child is known by their acts. And this is a fact without doubt if care is not taking concerning their acts at their stage, and then forms their destiny without knowing by their parents.

Parents must consider their children lives acts in all the time and take note of their doings every day and guide them of their doings. One of the reasons why children are vanity stands on their acts and they are thoughtless of whatever they are doing.

Their life cannot be managed by themselves except it guide by the mature person and those who have experienced life in the circumstance. The children must be guided by the way they should go, so that, at their age, they can cope with every situation.

Note the scripture: Proverbs 22: 1, 6, 15 A good name is more desirable than great riches; to be esteemed is better than silver or gold. Start a youth out on his way; even when he grows old he will not depart from it. Folly is bound up in the heart of a child, but the rod of discipline will drive it far away.

The children must be guided and teach. They lack the total choice of an idea but ready always to receive any acts impose on them. They are ready by any life wind blow on them and lack the choice of right from wrong. The youth are subjected to negativity.

They always make foolish things and are subject to any pressure, and have no choice. That is, they take whatever flashes in their sight and behave any manner of life set before them. Your child acts today will be the name of his or her destiny.

Parents are responsible for their children's acts and the manner they live. The children are like the mountain, they receive and respond to any sound heard. So, the parent must guide and to protect their children from any act or danger which can be results in their life ruin in the future.

12. The experience acts

Life experience is about understanding in life matters and the reacts of that life shows the maturity stage. The things done on earth have a way of doing. And there are lessons involved in the movie. There comes experience. The masters' key.

Life has stages. Through these stages their experience grows and act according. Life without experience is immature and fruitless. The experience acts are the life fruit that one has to do correct things and to apply for the benefit of others. That is, that person knows what to do and understand the results.

The experienced act is the best way to handle things in a matured way and the best way of doing things. When one has experienced in life, his or her management in life is secure and fearless.

Experienced produce care and the care produce security and understanding. The one who has experienced in daily life activities have a balance in life management and produce good result about life issues.

In fact, those people live without fear and make a prudent decision about whatever comes in life. Mistakes in life are the teachers that teach lessons of care which prevent the eternal damage of life and prompt us on the things without our knowledge to be well aware of.

In life, the weakest man with mature experience can live at least a better life with well balanced acts. But not all can manage life with the experienced gain.

It depends on the attitude of an individual who knows the laws of life and how it was managed by circumstance encountered. Many people have a lot of experience in life but not all can manage the trials in life and live upright. Experience teaches lessons of patience and in the practical way of doing things as well.

In life, the experience makes the difference in the capacity of the performances or responds to the mature acts, well known of individual who can manage than the other.

And without experience, things cannot be managed well. Means managers must be knowledgeable and practically know where to start life again when things go wrong.

Everyone needs to have some amount of experience in life; else life cannot be managed as well. In fact, every human being needs to have a skill which is the life food to survive and to have his or her being up to the point needed in the life journey.

The nature of our being was designed for activities. And the members of our being function by exercise, and through this activities knowledge is gain; and there comes the experience, which is the life wealth that protects us from enemies that destroys courage.

Note that, lack of experience brings a lack of competency. And the manner of that life becomes objection. Our life stages show how we should be patient, and manage the life step by step as the day goes.

Life is managed in days, not a moment. And it needs stages to progress, and that is how God created us to live and have the need at every stage which is equal to the age and manage it well. That is why hours, days and years are given to us to know what it means to have the best in life than ruin our life. Those who want things quick destroy their life and lack wisdom and knowledge about life. However, life in this world concerns bitter, good, bad, happiness as the results of sin. But for us to manage life as to the wish, depends on experience gain.

Life lessons bring development and bear the fruit of patient that represent total understanding. In life, the patient carries the key to success and opens fortunes at the right time. But the one who lacks experience in life can damage handover property and discourage by trials.

But the one who holds the courage through life experience withstands every trial. The correct management and the best act of life depend on the stage of knowledge gain through circumstance which that life has faced. And knowledge gain determines the weight of that experience acts.

In life, hardship opens many ways and enlightens the mind for good planning, and life progress through the weight of the lessons solved. Every human being needs experience in life to act well; else the life will be abused by circumstance. The youth need more to learn about life and be able to behave well. Their age needs many lessons and their parents must teach them about life matters to guide them for better stage management.

13. The impact of every action

Life is about actions and the result is the fruit that bears. The waves of the sea speak a lot and bear the witness of acts. Our first parents have brought deep damage to us through their acts.

Our hope shakes every day as the result acts. The testimony of every person stands on his or her acts. Every act carries all the answers equal to the stage of that life and no witness carries the weight than our acts.

Our life progress by the response to the laws governs nature and the acts are the advocate of a true witness who decides our stand whether to the left or right. The youth must observe their acts seriously and be careful of their movement.

The world we live has two options and the options have the reward which no one can escape, and it is a definite result of which we cannot do way, and it will be a home for everyone privileged to live the world, and everyone possesses the one at the end whether like or not. Every act makes a home and that is the reward of that act. Our acts identify the speech and the nature of that speech testifies the attitude of that person. Life acts impact a lot, and the result of that influence makes a home for us.

Let consider this scripture;

Mathew 18:7 Woe to the world because of the things that cause people to stumble! Such things must come, but woe to the person through whom they come!

People in the world have a lot to count, let's note that our actions are rocket bombs that destroy strong mountains and cause cracks to the earth and makes dust in the air for people to be affected.

Many of the youth acts cause damage and serious effect than they think. As the fire cause damage, so to the acts, we intend. We should not take things for granted, all manners of life has the result and everything deeds on earth will be counted.

Today's acts can affect tomorrow's destiny and how it was acted can cause eternal lose whether for you and to the others. We will be by judgment our acts whether good or bad. (Eccl. 12:14) whichever acts that cause someone to fall or make somebody short among his or her brethren will pay the penalty. Let consider this scripture again;

Mathew 18:6-10

6 "If anyone causes one of these little ones—those who believe in me—to stumble, it would be better for them to have a large millstone hung around their neck and to be drowned in the depths of the sea.

7 Woe to the world because of the things that cause people to stumble! Such things must come, but woe to the person through whom they come!

8 If your hand or your foot causes you to stumble, cut it off and throw it away. It is better for you to enter life maimed or crippled than to have two hands or two feet and be thrown into eternal fire.

9 And if your eye causes you to stumble, gouge it out and throw it away. It is better for you to enter life with one eye than to have two eyes and be thrown into the fire of hell. 10 "See that you do not despise one of these little ones. For I tell you that their angels in heaven always see the face of my Father in heaven.

We are more than what we think or see ourselves, God loves us than we know and cherish our life. All of us as human beings are dear to God, no matter what our condition or state; we are very dear to Him (God) and it cause all His life as a ransom for our life as an individual.

We must be careful of our acts towards our brethren and act according to what the law claim from everyone. That is, we should act decently in all our societies. It is very serious to act negatively and make people fall by plan and think that is okay.

Woe to you who intend to do that! It is better not to be in the world than to cause one to fall by your act. There is no way to escape from it and take it free.

Actions cause harm than any atomic bomb and destroy both the actor and the listener. We are born to be respected and have that matches life; there shouldn't be discrimination among ourselves.

Everyone has what goes with life and that is okay to make the community whole. Never value yourself than the other and think that you are up to the standard than your colleagues.

This attitude or act makes way for unforgiving sin to have a seat of people life and many people do not know how sinful it is to value themselves than the other. It is dangerous to exalt yourself and look down on others.

Every act in human life proves the stage of that person who acted and defines the nature of that being. The youth must act to respect and to act as to stand before God (The Almighty) and fear about their actions.

We all need to consider our actions and prove beyond doubt about the way and the manner we act because it will judge us in due time. Every word or act that proceeds out from any person has the effect which can cause damage or repairs the damage. And it is like the waves of the sea, it spread to the wide point of the wished end.

Men! We have a lot to deal with and to learn so many about life and it matters. The worlds we live is not there just like anything else that can be taking and go for free, but it is about counting and calculation for the correct answer and make the difference about what to choose and what not.

Every act count and the words explain the state of each being. Your acts witness about your true or falsehood and define your stage. Never deceive people by your sweet words and pretend like honey with all the sweets.

Further, many people deceive and act like lovers but not from the heart. Other people discriminate but pretend as devotees. All these acts cause damage to our fellow beings. Note that, your actions can cause somebody's death or life. Your appearance can bear witness about your attitude and make room for you. Our life on this earth today means nothing but our good attitude today can be meaningful on the next new earth.

All that is done on earth has the stand or position that bears the witness about the true or false motive behind the act and magnifies or decrease the beauty of it. Every situation in human's life witness about the starting point, and direct that life goal, and makes the lessons that it must be studying for better experience gain. Any act style, define the beauty or the ugly that holds the actor but the result makes the identity of that person who acted. Actions speak louder than any blast that man can make on earth. And if you act on anyway, you sound like dynamite that destroys mountains.

We must consider our acts in all manners of life and behave decorum. In a time of trouble, we must know how to manage ourselves and note that, in all conditions of life test our inner being and show the kind of persons we are.

In good times, know how to behave and bad times as well. The deeds we expose bears the total of our nature and for times that conduct takes shows the maturity of that performance. But the results of every act have the amount equal to the total weight that takes place. In all, our manners of life will judge us.

Never act without consideration; never eat without consideration, never dress as without mind, but be considerate in all the things about life and live humbly and get the best reward. This is about your life and not a joke!

14. Notes of consideration

Life is about considerations and the lessons which everyone must note. Today can be yours, but tomorrow will be someone else. Everything concerns life is about eternal joy or doom.

Never make merry without good and proper self-examination. Take the life as yes or no principle, everything more than this is evil. Never demand what belongs to someone else's or withheld his or her rights.

Make no difference among men or women in the basis of value the one than the other. Show respect to all people whether child; young or adult and cherish them as well. Do not show partiality in age among men or women but consider every age as due respect.

Be patient in all matters of life and be ready for good or bad. Plan correctly about the things you do and do the unique thing currently in the system and get the correct responses from the people around you.

Be prudent and act decency. Make Practice on good things and be kind to all people. Be ready to stand for truth and never deceive by your act; appearance or tongue. Be alert to help and at the same time work from the correct heart. Work hard but not to abuse yourself, do away laziness and keep your time as well. Make peace with all men and do your part to promote justice as well.

Buy the truth but don't sell, share with others about what you know is the best and never cover what will benefit others.

Give as a hobby but never hoard up what benefits others, share the little as well as the big. Be diligent about your work and search for other avenues that promote life to its best.

Welcome people with a good approach and share your joy and sorrow as well. Be creative and do the best one day at a time. Be the servant to others in all the service to men but not as door mart.

Work as a master but act as a servant and be humble in all your doings. Be gentle but not too gentle; be forceful as the law requires but not extending.

Life again consists of integrity; gentleness, forcefulness, preparation and good planning. We must be wise and at the same time as unwise depends on the condition not to cause damage to those who do not understand us. Let's set a good approach in all manners of life to promote human equality and to avoid differences. Let us show true love to all people and fear God.

Note this scripture;

Micah 6:8

8 He has shown you, O mortal, what is good.
And what does the LORD require of you? To act justly and to love mercy and to walk humbly with your God.

15. Constant crying

The world has changed because of sin, and the things are not as it is from the beginning. There are misplaces in nature and the beauty of the world has damage and the people are desperate. There is shouting for help everywhere hardly to hear or see but always pending.

Who will ask what is going on every day or who cares about, because everyone has a problem? But who cares about? Sadness sprang up within hours but who will deliver or ceases the anxieties. People are mourning each day and night but who will comfort and wipe their tears for them?

There is a saying each one for himself but God for us all. If so, I asked why God created a woman for man? There is no world without nature and there is no nature without the world, there is no man without a woman and there is no woman without a man.

We were created as social beings, that is, to form a community and live as one people on the bases of helping one another. In relation, man and nature cannot communicate as the same beings about sharing the idea.

The absence of a man in the world does not affect anything created. And the presence of man has no effect on nature, but if the woman wasn't created, man and nature cannot communication as social beings.

The most important thing in the world which is second to our life is communication. God created us as social beings and without communication, the world cannot move, everyone must consider that without communication no human being exists. And if there is communication, there's the world, if not, there is no world to live in. Why some human does not beings want to care for their fellow and even share what they have?

There are unseen agonies around the globe and the people are desperate for help of relief but who will care or ask or seek to help? People must look beyond the surface towards their fellow.

Many are suffering under the covering but who will care and help? Selfishness has become a wall to prevent one another to help the needy ones. Many lives have lost the right direction and strife for a good position but there is no sign of hope and shouting for help but there is no response. Others have lost hope and are crying for comfort but there's none.

Many people are losing their life because of lack of support. Who cares and who wants to assist? Good Communication is a remedy for heart and mental problems. Everyone was created to fit others.

Many people are mourning each day and night seeking relief to rest from stress bondage but remain the same. Men are there for men and everymen must assist each one.

Trees can't be our friends and the food cannot satisfy us completely with the living, but the correct social relationship can make us whole and have our being.

There are covering agonies in other relations, in marriages, choice of wrong partners makes bad communication and this devalues the marriage and its improvement. Mismatch couples are highly in pains and misunderstanding of one another.

Their marriage involves many struggles every day and night this remove happiness of each couple. Unsuitable communication in marriage can dig a bottomless pit for the community in whom they live. Many couples are shouting for help. The most annoy is married to a lazy woman or man who is not willing to work with a good heart to support the family and many have gone to this situation because of the lust of flesh and wrong choice.

Many are going through serious agonies because of the wrong choice of partners. It is better to marry to a foolish woman who is active in labour and willing to work than to marry to a wise woman who is lazy and not willing to work or not fair enough, this is most annoy and painful.

So let us find out and help the weak ones among us and relief pains of the needy ones who are always crying and are without hope of comfort, this will help us to have a better life for ourselves and to relieve the load of others. Men, we are each keeper!

16. The Nation agonies

A nation prospers under good leadership and good governance. Benefit from good planning. Bad leaders are a misery to the people whom they lead and are darkness to the state they rule. Leaders of ignorance are damage to their countries and their people mourn even when they do the right thing.

The unplanned leader destroys nation revenue and mismanages the nation's property. Leaders who lack understanding provoke even the thoughtless in the city.

Many countries are crying because of the lack of visionary leaders and incompetent rulers. A nation prospers through leaders who first take note of poor people, their success and care for their needs and also consider God first in all their doings. The nation becomes a curse when leaders seek their needs first and enjoy themselves only with their families and friends.

Many people have died because of bad governance and selfish leaders who seek their own, and the nation mourns when their leaders prospered. The selfish leader is a disgrace to the nation because every leader must first seek the people success and peace.

When the city agony goes away, it set up peace and justice, and then joy and success prevailed. When there is food, there's happiness and when there's hunger, there's anger. Further, when the nations have what it needs; the peace triumphed and everything goes on well, the sound people also increase for that nation.

The leaders of every nation must first seek the welfare of the people, and consider their needs to promote peace and justice for their nation.

17. The Workplace Agonies

The world is always increasing in wrong directions and things you cannot understand happening each day and night. Many People are suffering every day at their workplace and there is no mediator who will help solve their problems.

Work leaders and those who own jobs have made it hell to others who work with them. Misunderstanding goes on every day at the workplaces, managers, and their colleagues struggle and argues on some certain issues resulted in disorder.

Money has become everything of the day and even God to some people. So many people struggle for money every day and others find ways to have promotions in their workplace. And others kill some of their mates to occupy their position and to be promoted. Hatred without meaning goes on every day because of money.

Cheating grows in minute and war goes on every day, and the curses sprung up each moment. People who are low in position at workplaces are mourning every second. Cheating in payment occurs every month, some cry before receiving their money. Leaders delay payment of their workers and even become angrily to pay them. In fact, the world we are living now has reached its stage of destruction and peak of disaster in its state.

There is no truth whatever we are doing and people are cheating each other to gain their needs and there is no respecter of law. Rich people are increasing in wealth and the poor people remain the same.

Bribes increasing each day, there is mix-up everywhere and worries bulk up every moment and some are overwhelmed, and others die each second. Things difficult to comprehend are happening every day and night. Some people are a charm to be poor in a state for others to have wealth of them and some are bound to be speechless to cheat them not to prosper in life.

Many have been bought by food and charm to labour without rest and to gain nothing. Some people are also lock-up to be a servant until death. Others also have been assigned to be beggars and not to prosper in any work they will do but to suffer debts throughout their life. Very Strong agonies are going on in some people live each day and night, but who is to rescue and comfort them?

18. Agonies in Churches

Now Churches has become a money-making marketplace and show off what you have and get promoted. Today if you don't have the money you will not get any leadership position in the church. Discrimination is increasing in Christians churches today and unfair in dealing with others who are poor in appearance.

Many are suffering in Christian churches today feeling rejected because of poverty. Some are unhappy and feel ordinary because others don't want them due to their state. The true object of worship has gone out from the mind of Christians today because many of them are following the flesh.

So many of them are searching for worldly riches and its beauty but failing of the true worship. The Church members today don't care about themselves as it was at the beginning; the church has become a stand-alone by doing things individually.

Many church members read but they don't remember what they read since they don't practice what they read and forget even to apply what it requires from them and through this mistake, they let others suffer, in which if they do apply, it will be a benefit to others who around them.

The church has wasted a lot of blessings due to the waste of money fundraise and not properly use for the benefit of the members due. Many church members are in the sense of throwing away their money without benefiting anybody in the church or outside the church.

The church is always misusing the storehouse food which is to benefit the work of God and the proper way of using it. The storehouse food must multiply in each day to promote the work of God and benefit the members in and out, but what do we see?

Monies are raised to benefit nothing; there shouldn't be anything that is waste in the house of God which will not be a benefit to others. All monies raised in the churches should be multiply by investing it.

Now the church is so narrow in mind that, the monies raised go waste without multiply for other benefits. For the meat to be in the house of God always, the monies raised must be invested in the areas of productions, so that, there will be always food for the needy. As the church of God, we shouldn't waste the monies raised without multiplying it, by so doing, it will reduce the burdens of the members who are hard to have money for the offering. The church activities shouldn't be a burden to the members who are in the state of destitute.

The church in any way must find ways and means to reduce emergencies of giving's without a plan and this will show the maturity of that church and leaders who know their duty as God people.

The church that practices proper management in charity and follows the planning of donation in time will be greatly rewarded by God in due time and her members will be glad in coming to church always without burden.

The church leaders must teach their members in the planning of giving and by so doing; they will receive a blessing from God. The church must be a home of joy for all people who are weighing down with heavy afflictions and without hope of relief.

The church leaders must help their members who are jobless without intention but accidentally lose their jobs to be supported by the other members and to raise funds purposely to creating jobs for the members who are jobless and the members who have, must support the needy ones to build the body of Christ. The church must put aside fashions of the day which can create a burden to those who do not have money to afford it and rather be concerned in a modest dress to bring sanity in the house of the Lord.

Above all, church members must be treated equally and must be carefully deal with the member in the same manners. All things must be done beautifully and also in a rightful season.

There shouldn't be any favouritism in the church but equal love must rule and the priority is to save the hopeless. The church must be the river of love and the peace which quench the dry heart and revive the desperate in life.

Sometimes, the leaders in the church, wants the church members to appreciate them for their work, meanwhile, they don't know the real problems the members are facing. This is very serious that the leaders must be carefully considered, about what they have established concerning the appreciations they want from their members to do for them. Are they wanted to receive their reward on earth? Or wants God to reward them in future? Wherefrom this appreciation days in our churches today?

The leaders must be careful about the gifts they want from their members of which stands for no reason, which can result in a curse against them and their family. The leaders must be as servants not to demand any appreciation from the members or set date to be appreciated or to be giving gifts as their appreciation.

The appreciation must come from the free will from the people they serve and not to demand it. Your work will be rewarded indirectly but you should not seek for it or set your mind on any appreciation or even demand thanks from any of the church members.

They must offer everything from heart and freely serve their members and note that God will reward them. Christ serves with no demand for any appreciation from anyone and He is their example. Why today the leaders of the church want to be appreciated? Whiles, it is their duty to serve and not to demand, the one who serves needs nothing from the one whom they served but their reward will not fail as their service due.

Many are suffering in the church and they need a redeemer to rescue them from their miserable state. The church is the home of liberation to burden bearers and refuge for those who are chain by the devil. And why is the church today becoming a burden to others because of certain acts and demands? Failing in the duties required of them? Misplacing the leader's responsibilities? Demanding instead of serving freely?

The church leaders must very considerate about matters of their members and are ready to serve and not to demand. They must display a good example on how to serve their members and be their help in good or bad seasons.

They must do away equal in giving among the members within the donation or harvest sessions and cease the projection of tentative block among themselves and relieve the burden of destitute among them.

As Christians and leaders, we must put off measuring targets to our members in the donation and shun mention big amount in harvest sessions." Woe to the world because of the things that cause people to stumble! Such things must come, but woe to the person through whom they come!"(Matt.18:7)

Many poor people become unhappy during harvest time in our churches and these hours become a burden to those who don't have and to give. The church must stop the activities which cause others to stumble and to do things fairly for all those who attend church services and lets us do things beautifully in the right way, and God will bless us all in our doings.

19. Single Parent agonies

The man was created perfectly and relatively by God but sin has broken everything concerning him. Total happiness has gone out of the man and the real living has broken. The joy of communication has been stain by sin. Things are not in a position as it should and life has become part of its nature by the death penalty which is sure without the escape of any man who lives in the world.

The life cannot be without a woman for man and too, it cannot be full for a woman without a man. Every Man needs support to survive and to have his being. And as the scripture says, two people are better than one. And too, it is hard for one person to reach his or her goal without the support of someone.

In life when someone is left out he or she suffered and it is hard to live life without support. The circumstance in life has brought a lot of worries to man and life has become more burdensome to deal with. When your husband left you or suddenly death claim one of you, the other left suffered and life becomes worried about the one who lives and sorrows always fill the heart of the one left behind.

These agonies always develop when the one who lives remembers the dead one. If this happened, what should you do? And what will be your comfort? Always remember your creator and trust Him. Single parenting has a lot of worries in things done on earth and it is a struggle without explanation and people who have been in such situation needs careful attention and real support not by words but in action.

This world has changed to the worst part and there's nothing on it which can stay in it good state to the end. Many are suffering in the condition where no one cares about them because of their nature which is not to the standard as to what expected of those people who think they own everything.

These world troubles are individual feelings and no one in this world can understand the real pains of the other, so all pains are felt by the one who is in that condition and no one can feel the real pain but can show the concern of that feeling.

Single parenting needs proper concern of the people around him or her to free some of their agonies. Many are the human suffering but the one who suffers is the single who don't have assistant but the one who suffers the most is the single parent with more than one child and without a helper, this is very painful and worrisome.

As human beings, we need to look beyond the surface and search for the missing one, that is, we must find out the weaker ones and support them, those who need your support and encouragement.

This is the very duties we shouldn't overlook as human beings, if there is any concern, it must be looking beyond on how you see your brother or sister in the appearance and diligently find out the real condition about your neighbour. We need to support ourselves and be each keeper and receive blessings from God.

20. The agonies in old age

The Life hopelessness age or the condition you cannot escape and the supporting age of which every human being will pass through unless dying before or not born into this world and that is old age or the human ending stage. When men become old, they need support from the youth who are capable of doing.

The Old men must be taken care off and not to left isolation. In old age, men become like a child who needs the care to survive. They become helplessness and weak in strength, through this weaker stage brings a lot of stress which resulted in agonies beyond the margin.

Today people lack care of each other and that has led to forsake the old man and woman who brought us up. That is, Grandparents need to be taking care off more than what supposed to be.

When the trees are taking care off, life also prospered and prolong, so to the honour of grandparents prolongs the life of those who take care of them. There is nothing in this world so painful than loneliness and this is the situation of our grandparents today. Some families curse today is been isolated their grandparents and people don't know this knowledge about, so they even treat their grandparent as rag been left over.

Grandparents who are been forsaken agonies become a curse to their children and the nation at large. Grandparents need support and comfort every day if it is possible from their children and those around them.

We all heading towards our old age, if we neglect to help the aged, we will also be neglected. The youth must support the aged and care for them as they can.

Life today has become more difficult because of the growth of evil and it grievous results throughout the world. There is no love in the system of a man and there is no kindness among men, we all living for self and not for ourselves and there is no care among us again.

Loving the world and cherishing its belongings has covered the love for each individual and has placed hate among ourselves and also have resulted in more hate to grandparents who are weak to do for themselves and has brought much pain to them.

21. What your condition be in the end

Oh, is there anything in the world that can escape the coming day or is there a hidden place in somewhere men can loge from the day of reckoning? Have you ever imagine how this world will be in the coming day?

What will be your lot? And how have you considered about the coming day? I am always worried about the way we live in today's world. If you consider the history of this world and the calendar God has set for it, you can see that the days gave is over.

(See Daniel 7:44) "And in the days of those kings the God of heaven will not set up a kingdom that shall never be destroyed, nor shall the kingdom be left to another people. It shall break in pieces all these kingdoms and bring them to an end, and it shall stand forever", if you look at the history and what the bible is saying, means that, we are in the period of grace.

All the Prophecies has fulfilled, we are only waiting for the sound of Christ return. And here comes in my question, what will be your condition at that time of reappearance? Because of sin man conditions have changed and death has captured the state of human being. All kinds of disease have taken over the nature of our being. We are not in better condition as it was at the beginning of creation.

Things have changed from the state as it was at the beginning and nothing is perfect again as said by God at the beginning of creation. "God saw all that he had made, and it was very good. And there was evening, and there was morning—the sixth day". (Genesis1:31). Have you ever think of the situation men go in before death takeover? Some die prematurely, some die in sickness; others die in very old age and so on.

If you look at such conditions, and take it carnally, which of them is stronger even to stand when it comes to running for their life? This is the very condition we should consider much even when taking it as carnal. Which of those can even escape?

And if this is the condition of human being, how can we withstand the coming fire? Why don't you repent of your wrongdoings and make the correct step for your life? Take yourself as an old man or woman and consider your weakness or your state where will you stand, when it happens to run from violence in your city, what can you do for yourself? Now you can picture how horrible it will be when Jesus Christ returns. And I'm asking where will you stand? If there is anything we must consider, is the position of our future or our lot in coming days.

We shouldn't run after world goods and other belongings but we must consider our state tomorrow and nature by which we will find ourselves. The owner of this world is coming, what preparation have you done? Can you welcome Him? Will you be a son or daughter of Him? Will you be part of the life eternity?

Oh, my dear, if there is anything you must love; it is the home of infinity. This must be your first consideration and do all you can to have the time without end and repent now of your sins or do you want to suffer again after your death? You must escape this condition. Amen!

22. The agonies in joblessness

Many people are suffering in this world in a jobless situation not as they are lazy but it is the condition of change in era. But there's nothing in the world which goes on permanently but the situations which we go through are part of life that also help to mature in life we are living.

In fact, life is all about a job in terms and conditions of human and be a real being, it stands for working. But fortunately, there is a certain circumstance in the life that has brought some unexpected conditions which are not understandable to the human condition. Such a life is difficult to understand and totally deep to find out.

Today many are jobless and life has become unbearable to them and doesn't know what to do and even their state shows as dead because they cannot find themselves well among the living due to their state as jobless.

Living without work becomes lifeless. But living and not willing to work is the state of laziness. And that shouldn't be supported nor have pity for such a person. Many are in the dark stage, because of jobless and are worrying day and night for a better living. But what will be their state, if help from someone is absent? If there is a condition so tough and unendurable is the state of jobless.

Life is working and so life without work is dead. Let support ourselves and share together for the betterment of all human being. And the able ones must support the unable ones for their better livelihood, and relief the jobless from the oppression and let us have a good mind towards ourselves and support one another for at least enough living, and relieve the burdens of those jobless among us.

Who knows what tomorrow will bring and who knows the beginning of the King and who can predict the future situations among ourselves and what will be your lot in days coming?

23. Too much of everything

The world has become a competition every day. The one who has wanted it more and the one who hasn't wanted to have, and the one who doesn't deserve wants to deserve, and the one who is walking wants to run, and the one who is running wants to fly.

What are they seeking, knocking, and asking for and to what extent? Many have hoard but not sufficient to them and some are numbered up but still not in full to them. People are seeking every day but what are they seeking? We are competing here and there want the best even than the better. Who has become full of his or her demand?

What you need is not everything but what you need is sufficient in modest and not in too modest insufficient. Many want it more than sufficient in modest. The one who has power wants more than the limit.

The one who has strength wants to cheat everyone. The one who knows wants to ignore every opinion from others who haven't reached their standard. Money has become king in all human activities, due to this, if you don't have, your words are nothing before those who have, and this has brought the very desire of money in people in this world which have resulted in killings of our colleagues.

Money making is not sin but the condition in which we want to make it makes it worse. In this life, all that we are doing must not be in a condition which is very alarming to all those who are around us. Sharing something with people around must be in a good example. Cheating is in everything we do and that become bad to the one who did it.

All things that we are seeking for must be sufficient in modest, and the things we are seeking should not draw the attention of the people towards the seeking; else it will result in sin. Many people are suffering because of too much of things they have, and many of them could not sleep at the night or have rest in their bodies and even been depress of their condition of haven in abundant.

Things we are seeking must be in the manner of needful in time as expected. Even learning is very good, but too much of learning can destroy the correct sound mind.

We must be careful in seeking too ample things for our good; we should seek adequate not an overdose because life is not for us to seek the things anyway. A better life is to have sufficient in all things that are needful in due time and also the better life doesn't stand on things you have but it stands on the peaceful way sufficient as that life needs in due time. Why people want things way but not the peaceful way?

Many people want to be rich without proper verge and do not care about the outcome. Some also seek money without reason and others want it in countless. But what is the benefit at all? Everything in this world has its nature and the colour of its beauty that fit.

In life, God has measured for everyone the required needed for the living but to others is not enough or pleasing and they want it the way it will please them. But what will be the benefit, if that person loses his or her life?

My brethren, this world, and the world to come cannot carry the people who want all things in limitless or in too much. Mind what you seek for and care your future. All things are vanity and meaningless. Whatever man does, in the end, proves his destiny. Why struggle for all things selfishly?

24. Too much simplicity

This world was created without question, perfectly and beautifully made by God and there's nothing to question with? The life we live today has full of questions because of sin. The life we live should not go beyond what it should be expected and also not to be too less as it should be looking at.

In all, every life must be exceptional. Whatever life we live, if possible must not have questions and answers. Whatever we can do must be within our might and by doing it in reluctantly way, it becomes evil.

Things that we do must be equal to our strength limit and not beyond or less of our potency. God created us out of question and that must be our life on this earth, if possible. Every life which is contrary to the set principles becomes evil. How do we live our lives? Is it lesser than what expected or bigger than the demand?

The life that we are living must be up to the standard which hasn't any mark of negative appearance; if possible, it must be a sign for good direction for all other people in the globe. Our life must be uniquely live whether poor or rich. There shouldn't be the sign of short to disgrace our maker but it should be modestly in a quiet spirit pleasant to God.

25. The agonies in waiting

Many People today want things faster than the way it must come and never mind the manner of the result at later. Due to the way we want things in life, there become agonies in waiting. In fact, waiting is the life success heart which carries the whole channels of decent life ever live on the earth, and there are no other keys which can open the best for life than waiting for due time.

The fruit of patient brings all manner of progress and maturity. When the seed is cast on the ground, it needs time to grow, so to waiting which brings best for life. There is a big agony in Waiting due to our condition.

God created the world in series, on day by day to show how the things must be done by the plan, and not all things are done at the same time. God did this to do away work overtime, not that He could not do things on the same time but He did this according to the purpose of how Man will do his work according to the strength-giving to him.

God created the things of the world each day to teach us lessons of the patient because He knows what will happen to men when rushing in life. Many people don't understand life and how we should live. Life has sequence or stages of which it must follow and prosper. That could not be or else you end in ruin. Waiting for cause hot to living but at the same time make things well.

Many have made a mistake because of impatient in life and has resulted in damage that cannot be healed. Every stage has a procedure in life and that procedure cannot be put aside. That is, all age has the time of fulfilment in getting the things equal to that stage and it must suit the experience got. In law things must go as it should and not contrary, that is, life must go with the age and time.

Moreover, we cannot have all things at the same time and age. But we can have things according to the time set by God, and to understand the life best fulfilment. But we can have things at the right time and the right age. We need to wait for the right time at the right stage according to God purpose.

Why not have pains for the best things set up for you, and rushing?

In life, the patient is the measuring rod set for the best standard for the living. But it depends on the waiting to have correct fruit. There is a big pain in the waiting, but if that is enduring, makes things better. A good life is measured by the patient but the key that opens the best results is waiting. Why not endure pain for the best and wait for excellent? Oh, man!

26. Paying evil for good

We always experiencing new thing which is difficult to understand the cause and why it came. There is no vision of a man who can foresee or know the result. The sound is heard by striking a stone; all things done on earth have a good or bad result.

A setting Man was very fortunate to have special food from God, prepared by the angel whom he doesn't know him. The food was strange among the food the man knew always on his table. And it came to pass, the man called his brother to eat the food which he has got from the angel together with him.

The food was prepared with a lot of varieties of nutrient and well presentable in its appearance. So by eating the food together with his dear brother, the man who the food was prepared for, suddenly took the hand of his brother out of the food, which they were eating together. Then the brother whose hand was taken painted his cloth with the unwashed hand.

The stain became an identity of the brother whose hand was taken from the food. And this became a witness against the one who did that. After finishing eating the food, the man who the food was prepared for became nice in his appearance, enjoying good cars and house well furnished. But the brother lives nicely with that man who takes his hand and hasn't done anything against him but leaves the case to God.

What do you think about this incident? Meanwhile, the man whose hand was removed from the food was the one who the angel prepared the food for. But because the man whose hand was removed from the food wasn't there, the angel leaves the food to the man who was the brother of that man.

But because the rightful owner of the food wasn't there, the angel leaves the food to the brother who lives with. But the one who the food was left with making it his own and also became selfish by eating together with the brother who the food was prepared for.

The food was very sweet, so the man who the food was left with, plan not to eat again with his brother. What is your response to this incident? Meanwhile, the close brother was the one who helps the selfish brother to survive.

Moreover, the selfish brother was disabling to do the work. Unless his brother who nearby helps him, else he cannot do anything to survive. Never reward evil for good to the one who has helped you some time ago, else you will live to regret. Oh, what a world we are living! How will you answer this? Paying evil with good, let us be careful of our doings.

27. The flesh without bones

Lack of inner ability is the results in outer or physical inability. And not all human being can know right from wrong. Some appear nicely in stature but are knowledge less, fine but of no use, beautiful but active less.

The giant body sometimes deceives many people and let them admire vacuum. Knowledge and wisdom are not there for beautiful giant bodies but it is there for those who are willing to search for it.

People you will value will be people with valueless, and the people you think they are valueless will be the people with great value. And not all the obeisance people in society that are voted for can be ones who can solve the problems in society.

Sometimes people salute giants in society who lack wisdom and understanding. Not all the beautiful flowers have a good smile for the bees to use for their honey. So to some of the most respected person in the community.

Never margin what you think you have is the best than the one who hasn't what you have. But by using what you have; will determine the value of what you have. And never regard your best than the others but compare and make yours more useful for others to recognize it and praise yours than you think. You haven't encountered what you should; else you will not margin yours as of great value than others. Never praise yourself but let others recognized you about your competency.

Sometimes the little money you have can close your eyes from the best thing you must have. Not all nutrients are good for your health. But the one patiently prepared makes it wholesome. And also not all foods are good for the body, but the food prepared with sufficient nutrients makes a healthy body.

What do I want to say? Every human being in the world needs an education highly ordered by God. The only thing that God needs for his kingdom is Character! Without that, there is no other thing again for acceptance.

The flesh without bones is the deficiency of God nature in us or the character of God. And also by replacing bad for good or pretending to have the fabulous ability, but lacking good character. That is, beautiful but abhorrent in good manners. Never pretend to be good or force yourself to be good looking, whiles your stature holds your being. Your manner of actions determines your inner being, and the actions reveal your character.

Never deceive by your appearance but appear as simple and with no recognition. Never make someone know that you have what you haven't experienced before. But let them know that you are now learning.

Then you will have more knowledge and the best understanding. And serve as an example to others, then whatever you undertake to do, and then you shall receive a good reward. Remember to keep yourself in the position fit to standard, and never uplift yourself in the manner of deceiving others on the things you do not have.

But rather, be alert and prepare yourself for new things that bring improvement for yourself and others. The things that are needful welcome and help to society. Never appear as a light under the table but be the light on the table. So, you will be a benefit to others and the wealth of someone!

28. Why Stealing?

When you steal, means God is absent. Ask me why? In the presence of the owner of anything receive security. But the owners' absence makes less secure. Here people never mind the things of others but rather mind their own.

They regardless of others own and less secure when it is in the hand of the stranger. But secure in the hand of the owner. Due to this, other people want to steal and damage their fellow. Stealing is the act of selfish; murdering, falsehood, dishonoured, fornication, and regardless of God.

Those who engage in stealing are maturely selfish and deeply murderers and not human but wicked actors not to be entertain in society or everywhere around the globe.

It is highly and most dangerous sin ever, man has committed since evil arrived in the world. A human being received a strange destiny, which is a death sentence because of stealing what God hasn't permitted but man selfishly steals what was not permitted.

This act does away the Creator of this world and everything in them. Stealing means there is no owner of anything you came cross and also there is no one who created this world. As humans we shouldn't go in for what was not permitted for us, else you are thief and murderer. So whatever we are engaging ourselves in and not permitted by God, turns stealing and we mean it is there for nobody.

Stealing is now highly recommended among us, and some are promoting it every day and night in our society. It is going on in the house of God, going on in the schools, going on in the government institutions, in the marketplaces and everywhere around the globe.

What I don't understand among Christians is that those who called themselves Prophets, Pastors, Bishops, and so on, are engaging themselves in the doctrines contrary to what God has said and are highly recommend the forbidden ground to their followers. Some are into fornication; others are deceivers and so on.

These acts are all stealing and meaning God is not there for recognition. Those who are engaging in the act contrary to the word of God are thieves, and practising the unbelief of Deity who created the heavens and earth.

Some men are put away lawful marriage and fornicating day and night. This is the act of stealing because those women and men are husband and wives to others. So why are you engaging yourself in this act?

Furthermore, some are stealing with their pens; others are holding guns to threat and steal, all these acts undermined God presence, and shows unbelievers of God and the disrespect to Him.

If there is a curse in the world, it goes to those who engage in stealing, and other acts contrary to the word of God. Men, it is better not to be born than to be a robber.The entire curse rest on this act and those who involve in this act are doomed.

This world cannot be managed properly if this activity continues in the individual doing. This will lock the blessings of God to mankind. Many people regardless of their colleagues, overstep their belongings and take as theirs.

God created everything for a purpose and rule of law and principles. Don't abuse, because of your benefit and regardless of the rest other people.Adam is for Eve and Eve is for Adam, one man, one wife and one woman, one man. Never take other wives, because of your money and also never take other husbands, because of your beauty.

Not all things are permitted to use and moreover, not all things are good to use. So what was not permitted by God is not fit to use. Whatever it is, whether beauty or not beauty, whether precious or not precious, we must obey the word No or Yes! If we regard God, we will not steal. Why stealing?

29. Willpower and the choice results

Everyone has the will of a choice and the defense of life. There are boundaries and the area of living. If anyone misses or cross over the demarcation lines to the other territory without permission cause crash or damage to the other.

The willpower and the Choice is the act of good or bad response. It is hard for someone to break through the walls of the willpower unless the choice considered.

Nobody can have access to the mind. Unless it is allow by your willpower. Without your will, nobody can control you. That is, no one can access your area of living. If there is anything too powerful than powers in the world is willpower. In this world, if the life can be managed as well, it stands on the determination, that is, willpower.

Best life comes by choice and the key to success is willpower. All things are done by the ability we have but the correct application of it best done, stands on willpower.

In life we all move by the willpower we have, no one can force you to move unless you subject your willpower him or her. So in life, what you want yourself comes true. God gives us the liberty to move as we wish, He never forces us to do His wish but prompt us to choose a good path for living.

The result of your good or bad choice is the ability of your willpower. In all, we live by choice and have bad or good by willpower that we hold. In our nature, Mind and heart rule or have power than anything concerning power but the engine that controls its working ability is the willpower.

So all things plan comes from the heart but the recommendation stands on the mind or the brain. There is no place so secret than the mind and the heart. There is no wall so strong than the heart and mind of human beings.

The only bulldozer that can break this wall is willpower and the tool to impress the heart is the choice. So the interest of man in something comes by willpower.

Brethren, no power can imprison your power of imagination unless by your willpower approval. So, when we sin, let us accept that it is our will and the pretention of our choice. Many have fallen apart, because of choice and other things have been broken because of our will.

This world is going to an end, there is cry everywhere witness that. The world is running out, the world cannot recover herself again, the wall of protection is now in ruin, there is no good standing, the shadow of darkness are gradually piecing together, no light for better shining, days are now over, there is rumor everywhere, people are roaming here and there for better refuge.

There is no rest for human beings; our willpower has broken, because of the pleasure of the world, people are dying because of the bad choice.

We must hold our being and determine the good price of our being, never allowed the weeds to take over the heart. We must make the right decisions and stand firm because it stands on your willpower to progress and the choice to magnify.

We are almost home but the key to open the door is our willpower properly kept will allow our access to the entrance. Our choice stands on our willpower and that determined the state of your house for future living.

We must be careful about whatever we are choosing because it can be the reward of our destiny in the future. Everyone in this world has the lock of a better life and its keys.

No other keys can open that lock, except the key of that lock. That is, no one can break your lock or open your lock by any other key unless you give it out or permitted by you. Means, all influences and the powers that are contending cannot overcome you without your permission.

Men, the choice stands on willpower and your fate determines by choice and the result is in your hands. Where do you want to make your direction? Oh man, the power is yours. Make the right decision and live wisely.

30. What life's progress depends on?

Life is how you think it to be, what you will decide to do, the steps you take towards it through daily activities and the amount of time you invest into it.

'When wisdom entered into your heart, and knowledge is pleasant unto your soul, discretion shall preserve you, understanding shall keep you' (Prov.2:10, 11). Consider yourself to be like the sky light, reason like one determined to become like that, and it will come true.

The broken cord in your life can be rejoined; you can have your access to life again, by your decision. Do not think it's too late, just because you are old; rather, make prudent decisions to better your lot, even if it means starting all over again with something small. Be assured that it's never too late, as long as you have life.

There are much noise and more storms around the globe, and it is very hard for someone to hear you. However, if you will be bold enough to speak, your voice can be heard at the back of the storm. And it is your singular duty to make it possible for others to hear your voice. Note that the noise of life around you is very loud; in fact, it's louder than any noise you can think of. This means you have to be louder than the blizzard of life, which is a potential hindrance to progress in life.

Strive for your life's ambition purposed by God for your benefit and the benefit of others. Your new style of positive adornment can positively benefit the demeaned person in the community, and the new idea of creating something can be wealth for someone.

Be a good example and patiently seek wealth for your life in a lawful manner, for it will help you and others around you. Never be a burden to your family and others in your community; be a reasonable man or woman enough to do your part to make things happen.

You can never go forward unless you plan and act to be like that. So life's progress depends on fighting against the incorrect to replace it with the correct or bringing the lack to an end in life. Never think you will become successful when you fail to help someone. It is difficult to have a breakthrough in life if you do not make a move in that direction.

Create a job by your own effort and always think of its growth and expansion. Life without work is like sitting in darkness. Life will favour you by the purpose of God (Rom. 8:28). The circumstances you find yourself in are factors that propel your progress. This means that when some strange things come into your life, you must not consider them as the end of life.

So many people are out there, but *someone* is standing there. This suggests that the uniqueness of good behaviour can give you a beautiful identity. Life without Christ is life without hope.

Focus on the right things you are doing and do them well. Life without purpose is life out of the stage. Progress in life rests on life's purposes. You may be out of progress because you never aimed at anything. Never fear to progress because of circumstances. Press on to the end; never get tired of progressing. Amen!

31. Purposeful living

Every life must have a purpose. Life without purpose ends in vanity. In life, one must have an aim to guide him to make the right choices. Doing this consistently means that one has a vision. The end of a life of vision is the right results. Your purpose becomes the key that opens the progress of the life that you want to lead.

Every life succeeds by right purpose and progresses by right decisions. In this world, so many lives have been damaged because things are done aimlessly and haphazardly.

Your purpose must be accompanied by the right decisions and the right choices. Purpose leads you to bear fruit. Right purpose bears the right fruit, and bad purpose bears bad fruit.

Many people consider life as without rule and live it as they want; they never mind the outcome of such aimless living. Aimless living becomes aimless life and ends in fruitlessness. Having a purpose in life makes a human being truly human, and a life without purpose is already dead. Your decisions depend on your purpose. The Right purpose bears fruit based on positive thoughts and the bad purpose also bears fruit based on negative thoughts.

Your purpose shows the thought you have, and the life you live revolves around the thought you have. A damaged life is a reflection of the mindset of the person who lives such a life. Fruitful living shows the purpose of that life, and the banner of progress stands on rightful decisions. So many people live without thinking; they live aimlessly.

Every life needs a purpose and right decisions to get good rewards. Never live without the purpose. Make sure, however, that you live with the right purpose, right decisions, and right choices.

Set the right goal, live by the right choices, watch your doings, and get ready for the right rewards. God will help you to live by the right aim, good decisions, reasonable ends and great rewards for a better future. Think, think and think well.

32. The competition of life

Life without war is life out of the stage. So life with war is the life of progress with an aim. Nobody can reach a high stage without a purpose coupled with industriousness and perseverance. God created everything in its perfect order. Why then has life become war every day? And why is a life not easy at all?

There are enemies of progress and these enemies are you, sin and the evil angel on your path every day. But, by the grace of God, You can be who you want to be if you make Him king over you. Every life starts with zero; true life depends on God for better fruits.

Life offers a variety of lessons at every stage. The lessons may come with happiness, tragedy, sorrow or mourning. All these are benefits of life because of the situations and conditions in which the world is.

Nobody in this world is without hope. But you cannot attain your aim in life unless you have a sense of purpose. Life is sweet when you have what you need, and it is bitter when you lack your needs. Never grow weary in your pursuit; forge ahead to get it. Your achievements lie on the ability to handle and utilize a purpose. You can handle your purpose by taking appropriate measures. Nobody in this world can take it easy! I mean no one can possibly achieve his or her needs without hard work. So many people in this life want short-circuited lifestyle to enrich themselves. But that is dangerous, even when it becomes possible.

They end their lives suddenly. Be patient with whatever you want in life and with whatever you do. By patience and longsuffering, you will reach your destination.You cannot go forward whilst you are still standing. Move and you will reach your destination by determination. Be active in your movement and you will reach your stage. Do not slack or stop for any reason. Watch out on things that may cause you to slow down or stop. You are one out of thousand; there is none like you. That is, see yourself as a unique person. What you have and your position are different from those of any other person. Appreciate what you have – even if it is little – and guard it. Never lose hope but be grateful to God for what you have.

33. Doubling your portion

You should not be narrow-minded; search for other opportunities and add up to what you already have. What do you have? What is your gift? What is your interest? What do you always do? Ask yourself these questions and others. Then start with what you have little by little – do what you can about what you have.

Also, develop positive attitudes towards what you have and gradually multiply it little by little. You can never multiply your portion with idleness. Invest time and resources into what you have. God has given human beings gifts, and these gifts are at your disposal too. Move by the confidence with what you have been given; appreciate it. Having had your portion; you need to move confidently towards your goal. Your gift is your tool for daily living, and you are to account for it by the way you use it. Never joke with your gift. God expects something big out of it. What you have – whether small or big – is what you deserve.

Work with it, and it will bear fruit in the future for your benefit and the benefit of others. It is then that you will be regarded as a good servant.

34. Your condition today

How do you respect the time and its movement in this life? How do you manage your time? Your respect for time reflects the situation you are in now. Your time will never change the condition of your situation unless you respect it as you move forward. So respect time whilst you have life. Note that time is life.

So many people in this world have become poor because they have little or no regard for the time given to them by God. You will be victorious by keeping your time in every situation. Nobody knows what will be the condition the next time. So be prepared at each time and each moment.

Your time conditions are the situations you are in. That is, the reward of your time predicts its condition. Your condition today shows what you did yesterday. And that is your reward for the day. Respect time as you move on in this world. Your condition today is the result and the fruitage of what you did yesterday.

35. The rotation of life

Every life starts from a point and that point is the beginning of the life race. Your life records depend on your actions and behaviour. Every action of your life determines your success and defeat.

Every act of your life has fruits to bear, and these fruits bring your destiny. Destiny brings your real character, and that is the result of your life.

Whatever you do impact your life. You cannot hide anything in this world and still walk freely. The rotation of life will ensure you get back to your threshold.

Do right and you will harvest right. You can never cheat anyone; time will tell. As the world or earth rotates, so also the life you are living. Watch out! Every action returns to the actor, and the result is the reward to the one who acted.

36. Watching your thoughts

Your thoughts are your actions, and your actions are your thoughts. Also, your thought gives identification to the eye in all situations – whether good or bad – and gives signals to the whole face.

Bad thoughts can damage your life, stop your inner joy and demolish your real understanding. Your movement in life, sometimes, shows your thought at that moment. Your fears, your joy, your boldness, your willingness, and your competency stand on your thought.

You will not be well developed unless you have the right thought. What you think about determines how you behave. Your thoughts influence your speech, and your language gives an identity to you as a person. Your speech shows your thought. If your thought is right, your action will be right. The bad speech shows your thought.

Actions are the result of your thought. Good behaviour is fruit of right thought. Right thought brings peace, good health, and happiness to you. Your progress depends on the right thought. Your thought defines your personality, and that determines your stature as a human being. Whatever you do – whether good or bad – depends on thought. Your good works are your thought, and your bad works too are your thought.

Your thought will determine your life span, and your life span is the result of your thought. This result could be a healthy or weak body. That is, your state as human being rests on your positive thought, which makes you a real human.

Your sorrows depend on your thought; so does your happiness. Being sorrowful or happy depends on your thought. Watch what you think, for it determines your state as a human being. Think well. Your desire for right thought will let you think well.

37. The result of the attitude

Attitude is your reaction towards everything you do or your willingness to act. Your state today is the result of your attitude yesterday.

Your attitude is the key to open your success. How do you, welcome people? How do you welcome your work? How do you do your thing? How do you feel when it comes to working?

What are your reactions to work? How interested are you when it comes to working? Your response to work informs the amount of your wealth. Your willingness determines your state.

Attitude brings about the wellbeing of every situation of your life. Behaviour is a product of an attitude, and your actions are results of attitude.

Life cannot be whole without a good attitude. Considering your attitude will lead you to a good position, in order to please God.

So many people in this world have become miserable because of their attitude. Your feelings are not always right but your feelings can bring you up or down, and this is influenced by your attitude. Your attitude can make you benefit; it could also land you into trouble. Your situation is your attitude page, and that page is your reward.

38. Your Dreams are Your Secrets

Every dream is the real focus of your life's direction. Living without a dream is like a dead person, who does not know where he or she is. Dreams are life's purposes or aims.

What you dream about is your intention, and that matters a lot in your life. A dream is a spiritual guide for everyone in this world. It also serves as a help.

Never joke with your dreams; it is about your life. God speaks to you through dreams, and it is a secret concerning you and others. Numbers 12:6 says 'When there is a prophet among you, I the Lord reveal myself to them in visions, I speak to them in dreams'. Visions are keys that open the doors of your success, and dreams are your reality.

A dream must be considered carefully. It is the projection of life and the guide of destiny. You can develop through your secrets. You can be brought down when you reveal your secret. What is hidden is what no one knows apart from you. When you reveal your dreams, others will know your secret. What you do in secret can determine your life in this world. What you dream about will be the condition of your day.

Never reveal your secret to others; your dreams will expose you to others. The dreams are your light that shows the direction you should go. Consider your dreams as you move along in this life.

Let your dream answer your beautiful secret, which is your reward. Your dreams are your stages of tomorrow, and that pays you, as you move on in this life. Your dreams define you and the situation you will be in. Dream big and consider it.

39. Giving; an act of investment

Invest by giving to the poor, who cannot pay you back. Many people want to succeed but fail to give; they have little or no regard for giving. Proper investment, than any other investment, comes by giving to the poor.

'Throw your bread into a river and you shall reap it in the future' means you should invest by giving out what you have and at the right time, you shall receive it. Every giving has a blessing key which opens another opportunity for more blessing to come into your life.

It is God who first gave and humankind followed suit. Without giving, life becomes empty or as dead as a non-living thing. Giving is a life survival fruit, which bears a blessing to the giver.

We must consider giving than anything we do in this world, as life goes on because it's only giving that holds the keys of blessing. Many people are in this world out of blessing because they do not consider giving or do not want to give.

Every giving must originate from a correct heart and that will bear uncountable blessings into the giver's life. Giving to the poor is more blessing than anything in the world that concerns giving because you lend that to God.

That is a surer investment than any investment in the world. Give and it shall be given to you with good measure into your bosom. Never stop giving; continue in giving and hope to have it again. Amen!

40. Learning from your teacher

Your conduct becomes your teacher. In life what you study becomes your behaviour. And how you behave is what teaches you. You become what you study.

How you behave becomes part of you, and that is your character. What you always do is what you always know, and what you know becomes your understanding of what you do.

What you always do indwells you, and what indwells you is the fruit you bear. Your behaviour becomes rulers that bring blessing or curse into your life.

Your good behaviour is your wealth, whilst your bad ones are wrecks, and that is your reward. You must be careful with how you behave, for that brings your blessing or curse.

Your behaviour identifies you as a person, and that presents you to others. Your presentation becomes your personality.

Practice what is good, and you will be good. You become a master by starting as a servant through practice. Practice brings lessons, and these lessons bring studies. Studies bring creativity and creativity brings wealth. You must be careful with what you bring out, for that leads to your success or failure.

41. What laziness brings about?

Laziness has great consequences. It is better to be very hungry than to eat food prepared by a lazy woman! Your life's progress depends on what you are willing to do – what you love to do or what you are interested in doing. Every human being develops by working. Active work becomes beneficial to every human, and that is what God created humans to be, without which life becomes lifeless and meaningless. Everybody – whether abled or disabled – in this world must work. That is how God made it. You cannot do away with it. But when someone is not willing to work, it brings a curse to him or her. Laziness results in poverty. A lazy woman is a catastrophe to her husband; so is a lazy man to his wife the man. Never cherish laziness as you move on in this life. It's better not to work than to lazily work. Inactivity is a disease. A lazy woman can poison the family with her lazy food. And food prepared by a lazy woman is equivalent to food already in a refuse dump; it can't attract or be cherished. A lazy person who is not willing to work seriously in life becomes unattractive, and that results in poverty.

42. Kings but servants at their beginnings

In life, those who will succeed truly with the help of God suffer as their life progresses. This is true. They are those who seem to be without hope. Kings in this world appear like servants.

They start as land without water, trees in the desert and are unrecognized. Some even look unattractive to be respected, without hope of a better position, not appealing to be remembered, not worthy of hospitality.

Life sometimes becomes very difficult for such people. Despite all these, they are kings in opportunities, mighty in wisdom, creative, and very open. They are keys that open great doors for their communities.

Sometimes, these people start without any base. Their lives become worse for them to be able to succeed. That is, they appear as not hopeful of having anything which will help them to succeed.

In this life, people with hope could become hopeless, and people without hope could become heroes. Nobody knows what life will be. Never think you have more prospects than others; people you think do not deserve any fortune may be the ones who get better things. People who may not deserve any fortune, in your estimation, could have more than you can imagine.

People who are treated badly are the ones who succeed in life; those who are treated fairly may not find themselves in a good position.

Be careful not to treat others badly, for they may be kings in the future. Who knows the future of a servant? Some servants become kings in this world. Whoever wants to be great must be a servant.

43. Human condition

Your nature is not certain. What is more important to others may not be important to you. But certain things that are not important highly regard. Men waste their time on the things that cannot bring them eternal life. People value the dead over the living. Men have put the Giver of life into a second fiddle instead of the first fiddle.

People spend more time to make preparations for the dead than they do for living. They gather for unnecessary things instead of necessary ones. Evil acts are given premium over good ones. The dead are given more attention than the living. People trust in fake things rather than genuine ones. Foolish things are given more consideration than wise ones. People endorse evil things to the neglect of good ones. Arrangements are made for weeds at the expense of seeds. Sand is dug for; not gold. People seek the devil instead of God. Unhealthy foodstuffs are hunted for. People blame others instead of themselves. Humans need Christ and his Spirit to overcome these weaknesses.

44. Valuing little things

Every life starts with a few steps and these few steps bring the growth of that life's journey. Every step that you make is the combination of gathering life into a whole. The beginning of every life has a pace. Therefore, you need to measure every step that you take by proper progressive measures; that is, the laws governing its growth.

Every speech, walk, look or word makes life good or bad. There is nothing big in this world without a small beginning. All lives start on the zero points. And that zero points is the foundation without hope. That is, nobody can tell what life will be, from scratch. Life's progress is the combination of the little things that we do. Every little thing has value for making that life's growth reach its stage.

Never disregard the little things you are doing, for any little thing you do introduces you to bigger ones in the coming days. Faithfulness in the little things you do makes way for greater things. All the things that we do must be noted, but the little ones must be cherished than anything else. He who is faithful in little things handles bigger ones. A little drop of rain also makes a stream. So the little time spent on little things bears much fruit.

People make fun of small things which actually must be seriously considered. When you can do bigger things on time, never joke with doing the little ones faster, for that can disgrace you.

Little things must be handled with care because the little ones are the difficult ones that you cannot overlook. Little things can do thousands, whilst bigger ones may offer only one. Talent has more to do than many talents that others have.

Never disregard the little thing you possess; value every little thing in this world, whether good or bad, big or small, for any of them can predict your stand tomorrow. Every little action has a lesson to teach.

Little by little, life grows; little by little, things are gathered; little by little, blocks are joined to build a house. Appreciate the little you have; you will be considered great by your faithfulness in the little ones you handle well.

45. Keeping what you have

Never say it is finished whilst you have life. Many people in the world today rush to have other things more than to pay attention to what they have. What do you know?

What do you always do? What's within you? What do you have? You need to find answers to all these questions.

We always lose what we have because of what we want. That is, people want money instead of work. People want to make wealth fast by avoiding their responsibilities. People want to be richer than they want to work for what they want.

We should not labour to be rich; we should labour to be responsible. People forget what they have because of what they want. That should not happen.

You need to work and be paid. Let the payment be sufficient for you, because that is what you work for. Never lose what you have because of what you want. What you have is your wealth. Work with what you have, and that becomes you. Consider what you have and care about it.

Human beings are classified by what they have, what they do and know. Develop what you have rather than what you want, and you shall receive what you want as well as what you have.

That is, know your talent, work on it, and you shall receive your wealth or success. People know you by what you have, not what you want. And that brings your reward.

Never replace your life with your wants. Seek not the riches of this world to the neglect of your Maker. Work on what you have praises your Maker and glorify Him always.

Never lose your integrity because of what you want; your gift is you and what you have is your identity. It is better to walk on a rough road with patience than to walk on a smooth road carelessly.

In life we must be careful how we live; we should not rush to get things easily by unlawful means; we must be careful and have what we need with patience. Driving on a curved road needs much care.

Similarly, life must be carefully lived. In fact, life cannot be straight, no matter what you propose.

Also, life is not as easy as some people want it to be; it is tough like swimming on sea waves. Be careful how you live your life. Why die before your time?

Every life is a great opportunity that lasts temporarily. There is no second chance in life; when you die once, that is all. So live it well, else you will lose eternity.

46. Position yourself well

Deception has been the order of the day. One deceives another by pretending to possess some skills. Another deceives his fellow by claiming work titles for which he does not have any skills. Such a person pretends to be skillful in a certain work.

Some people have taken some acquired knowledge and skills for granted whereas they do not have any knowledge concerning that field. Some people depend on other people's skills to survive.

In life, some people appear to be what they are not and pretend to know what they do not know. Some even eat on tables which are not theirs; that is, they use somebody's certificate to have wealth.

They stand on the knowledge of others to gain their wealth. Such people exude false appearance. Life's circumstances will reveal their lack of the piece of knowledge that they pretend to have acquired.

Also, pretenders use names of others. That is, the use of somebody's acquired skills as theirs. Some fail to acquire skills for living. They only want to steal somebody's skills.

In life, you cannot always deceive another person, to have your wealth; you may succeed for a little while but the laws of nature will expose you.

It is sinful to make yourself known for knowledge or skills you do not have. For instance, people claim titles, like Pastor, Doctor, Engineer, and Contractor and so on, when in actual fact they are not.

This is criminal yet some people engage in it; they do so to gain money. Your fake title will lead to a fake position and that fake position will lead you to an empty stomach in the coming days.

In this world, especially Africa, work is given to incompetent people instead of competent ones. It is not surprising that in the course of time they are exposed and they become fools. Titles are nothing except they are accompanied with skills. You cannot continually cheat people with your title; you will be exposed.

Never feign who you are by conferring titles on yourself; time will reveal your foolishness. Live on your own hands, not those of other people.

Acquire skills for your benefit; do not depend on somebody's knowledge to have your food. Use what you have to earn other things instead of depending on the earnings of others.

47. Beautiful for nothing flower

Adam was more privileged than his children. It was possible for him, the first father, to have life eternal than his followers but he prevented it.

Today, we are in a situation where everlasting life has departed from us forever but people in this world struggle for all the world's goods. Selfishness has taken over our state; we chase the world and its goods, which can never give eternal life.

Our condition as human beings is in the state which cannot escape death. You can add up to your body – but you cannot add up to your life. You can add to your life through Christ.

Food is profitable to the body but when the body dies, food is no more beneficial to it. You can fill your body with food but you cannot add anything to your life. Why then do you want to fill your body with food, which is temporary?

You cannot pick everything for yourself when you know it is going to be a waste. And you cannot also waste everything. Appreciate the little you have and let others also get some. Because you will be a waste, allow others. Let others have it. You cannot take all for yourself. Beautiful flower, but there for nothing! Beautiful flower, but not lasting! Beautiful flower, but there for a moment!

You are no more, even when you are living. And you cannot be anything when you die. You are there as a stream without source but a flood of rain only for a moment.

Why are you taking all of what is there for all of us? Beautiful but momentary, beautiful but profiting nothing to the world! A human being will be a waste, so don't stress yourself to get everything.

Our situation is not as profitable as expected; that is, God created us to be more than we currently are. Our condition is with hope and without hope.

That is, sin has become our decision-maker, and it decides our destiny. We should not waste what is left for us. Some people are so selfish that they want everything in this world for themselves only. That should not be the case.

You can become a hero on earth but zero in heaven. Why are you taking all for yourself? We are in a situation whereby we can die at any moment. Due to this situation, we must be careful about whatever we are doing. We must be watchful.

48. Tree among trees

There are unique things in the world. A beautiful character bears unique fruits, and a unique fruit identifies the tree that bears it. Good behaviour identifies a person that has it; so does bad behaviour.

That is, self-description doesn't make you a good person. But a trial time describes your beautiful being. Every tree has a shade and that shade identifies the size of that tree. This means that your appearance defines your identity.

Every tree has its branches that make the tree whole. Every human being can be described by how they talk, walk, dress. A tree that can withstand strong wind determines the state of that tree. Likewise, a beautiful character is tested by circumstances.

Many people in this world sometimes pretend as without fault in appearance. They pretend to live as if they were in heaven but they are as bad as the devil. Good trees bear good fruits; so do bad trees. A beautiful character cannot be bought or sold. However, it can be a choice. Living among trees is the choice of accepting good character traits; that is, the unique identity of a person living among many people in a certain area.

Your identity is the character that you reveal to others, and that brings your beauty among them. You cannot deceive anyone by wearing the adornment of a man or a woman when you are not one; your shape will reveal your false appearance. A bad smile makes a face change from its good state; so does a bad character identify a person's behaviour.

You can never walk by a pair of shoes that is not your size. Similarly, you cannot pretend to have a good character; the laws of nature will reveal you to the public.

You become good by choice and you become bad by choice. Trees that have good shade provide shelter for many animals; so does a person who is friendly and has a beautiful character.

Your actions will identify your good or bad character traits. Be a good example unto others so that those around you will glorify your Father in heaven. This may endear you to them as well. Your unique appearance brings your glory and makes you fit for a place of honour.

Be cautious about the way you act, regardless of your beauty. The good life comes with good behaviour; good condition comes by correct actions; correct actions bring good character, and good character brings a unique identity.

People of this world, sometimes, pretend to have good character traits. They pretend they hold the keys of goodness. But the dead cannot come to life again. To have a good character is not necessarily by the effort you make, but you must be fully willing to have it.

All trees in this world grow by the water absorbed from the earth; so do human beings who are willing to have good character. Character establishes the position of every human being.

The good character brings about good destiny. That is, willingness to have a good character will do you good for life, and it can be your fruit forever.

49. The Worker's due

Life is work, and working is living as life demanded. Our rewards are received by the work that we do. That is, every work has a reward attached to it.

Every worker deserves to be paid according to the work done as soon as possible. And that payment is the life gift for every worker. Our work in this world is a life establishment tool which cannot be avoided, in order to survive. That means we cannot have life without work. Work is life and living is working.

Life without work is lifeless. We work to survive; we do not survive to work. We eat to survive; we do not survive to eat. So life is about work.

Accordingly, every work needs to be rewarded. We work for our improvement. We also work to have good health. Work without reward is not work. We work to progress; not for our enjoyment. We work for rewards; not for the void.

Everyone who hires a worker must pay him or her in time. Never avoid the payment, when the work is done by the hired hand. Every work needs an immediate reward – payment.

Never deprive the worker of his or her payment. That is, give the right remuneration for the work done. Every unpaid work done brings a curse. Also, delaying a worker's pay causes great harm to the employer and the employee.

A nation improves by sticking to the correct time of payment by the government. When a government delays the payment of workers, it results in a curse to that nation.

'Never take advantage of poor and destitute labourers....You must pay them their wages each day before sunset, because they are poor and are counting on it. If you don't... (Deut. 24:14, 15).

A hired worker needs to be paid promptly; no delay must be entertained. Delay in payment results in curses. Note that whether the payment is made later or not, a curse has been evoked.

The doom of Africa is cheated and delays in payment of workers. When someone needs your help, never delay to give it when you have it.

Never delay the payment of your workers' salary; making prompt payment of salaries evokes God's blessings; no curse is attached to it.

50. The reward of cheerful words

Our world was created by the word of God. Every word has a fruit to bear. Without a word, life becomes lifeless. Our existence came by a word out of God's mouth.

A cheerful word brings development, and every human being develops by hearing a word of cheerfulness. Our life develops with words of motivation. The words we hear result in something good or bad in our lives. Words could provide something good or bad.

All our life's progress depends on the words we hear or speak. Good words make a heart cheerful; bad words are discouraging to the hearer. Some pieces of news can end somebody's life.

Human beings are known for their words. Our life's progress, sometimes, stands on words of motivation. Words of comfort give strength to everyone who hears it and moves to progress. A bitter word puts faith off and discourages the hearer.

In life, words of comfort encourage movement and make a life improve. In fact, life without words of motivation becomes unbearable. Everyone must encourage himself or herself with words of hope.

The word of God says, 'for I know the plans I have for you... they are the plans for good and not for disaster, to give you a future and a hope' (Jeremiah 29:11).

This scripture gives courage and hope. We must be careful about how we talk to others in our conversation. We need to speak words of hope to ourselves and encourage each other.

Another scripture says 'Fear not, for I am with you, and be not discouraged...' (Isaiah 41:10). These words uplift confidence and the courage to move on, whatever the situation may be. Words of comfort give hope.

To overcome life's circumstance depends on words of encouragement. Faith comes by hearing a word and hope also stands on the word predicted. In life, words help us grow, overcome difficulties, or fall. If God had not spoken, this world would not have come into being. Heaven and earth were brought into being through the word. So life depends on words for survival.

Without words, life would be lifeless. A word is a life-giving oil. Every word uttered must bear fruit for life. Our lives cannot develop without words. Decision making stands on the words we hear. Every word must be uttered in carefulness.

Life without words of comfort is life without hope. Always speak comforting words to yourself. Every word, whether written or spoken, has a certain unique action for life or death. We must, therefore, watch our speech. Our words are the seeds that grow to bear fruit. So we should speak good words to ourselves and others.

51. The greatest disadvantage

Life's package includes advantages and disadvantages. Our life in this world has questions and answers, because of our sinful nature.

Many people deceive themselves with false representations of themselves. Every human has a sinful mark. All humans need a power outside of them to overcome sin, which controls them.

In this world, there is a disadvantage, which should not necessarily be. Many people who follow Christ, and for that matter are Christians will not make it to heaven. Why? They misrepresent themselves in character.

So many people seem to be wasting their time by following Christ because they will not go with Him when He returns. And those people are the most disadvantaged in this world. They follow Christ but are not for Christ.

Many have taken the name of Christ but they are not true followers of Christ. Having time with Christ in his church does not necessarily offer one the permission to enter into heaven.

Christians who do not have the right attitude towards God are wasting their time in His presence, for it will benefit them nothing. That is the very thing that will happen during the second coming.

So many people in our day mention the name of Christ but are not for Him. Some have taken the name to make money; others take the Name, because of other personal benefits.

If someone thinks he is following Christ and he is not doing so in truth, he deceives himself. Many people will not go to heaven because of their stomach. Today's so-called Christians have sidelined the will of God but still, call themselves Christians.

Not all who call on the name of Christ are candidates of heaven; candidates of heaven are those who are willing to fully honour His commandments and faithfully follow Christ.

There is nothing in this world which is so dangerous than taking the name of Christ but not in truth; it would be better for such ones if they were not born into this world at all. Faithfulness to God brings true living; true living brings good character; and true character rewards great destiny. Never deceive yourself by taking the name of Christ without any desire to do his will.

Many professed Christians do what they like and not what Christ likes. Why call on the name of God when you do not desire to do His will? You are not a Christian if you do so.

The greatest disadvantage of the Christian would be to find himself in the lake of fire. Be a Christian in the true sense of the word, and do not just profess to be a Christian.

52. Considering bad times with good times

Humans, sometimes, forget themselves and fail to consider their condition – death – which has come to stay until the second coming of Christ. Enjoy life but consider bad times.

Our nature does not last as it should be. We forget our being when life goes on well. We always forget our condition as dead beings. Good times are characterised by happy moments, and happy moments cause you to forget the bad times ahead of you.

When things go on well in life, we even forget God, who created us. We always enjoy life, when things go well. When humans become rich, we even forget to seek help from God.

Enjoyment of life can cause damage to the mind and reason as well. Good life worries less of things around its environment. That is, it does not fret over those around.

Enjoying a good life may give room to pride if care is not taken. People forget themselves when they have fun. Sometimes, when you have money to purchase anything you want, you don't care how much it costs because you have more money.

It is important to consider bad times too. When you have money, sometimes, you don't mind what is coming. You, sometimes, do things the way you want, whether it's good or bad.

It is interesting that, when some people get money, they don't respect again. Pride takes the position of their being, and they, sometimes, speak harsh words to those around them.

Those who have not experienced bitterness in life pride themselves in what they have; they forget that dark day may be ahead of them.

Nobody in this world will get the opportunity of enjoying only 'good days' in his or her life without encountering any seeming misfortune. Life cannot be fair only, so we need to consider the things we do in this world.

Life is mixed with good and bad experiences. All things can be ours but all things cannot be yours only; we are in a world of inter-dependence. It is not good enough to enjoy life all alone without helping others who do not have.

Consider when you have what you need and be mindful of how you handle it because nobody knows which day is a disaster? Enjoy life as you have but consider your movement, because this world cannot be yours forever.

Be mindful of all your doings; your life must be beneficial to others. Refresh others and others will refresh you. Be humble, lest you stumble and crumble and lose hope.

53. Make use of every opportunity

Never waste time when you have a chance to do something. Do what you can every moment and never stop progressing. Always enhance your knowledge, if possible. Never give up, no matter the circumstance; press on to higher heights.

Life is hard but it's better when you have what you need. Time is life and life is time; never joke with your time; do good things, if you have time.

That is, seek other opportunities which can bring you wealth. Too much work can destroy but too much idleness leads to poverty. Do enough work but don't overwork.

Be faithful in your work; do not slack in any way. You will have what you need by working hard, and your reward will be full.

Always learn good things and practice them. Never leave your good deeds; be a good example to others.

54. Living as if all things were against you

Sometimes, life is as if you were dead but still alive. It, sometimes, becomes dark unexpectedly. Other times too, it appears that you are not part of life; you feel as if all people have rejected you.

It becomes unbearable and difficult to live. You feel lonely, whether you have a husband, a wife, children or friends. Life, sometimes, becomes bitter than the term 'bitterness'.

In life, sometimes, the light becomes darkness for you, and you wouldn't know what to do or where to go. Sometimes, you feel dead even though you are still living; life seems hopeless to you.

Life becomes very difficult; people live on survival skills. Happiness becomes sorrow and mourning. In times like these, never let hardship put you down or discourage you. Every man or woman born into this world is already victorious because of the opportunity to live.

God has given us the chance to know him, who created heaven and earth. And this opportunity is your reward for you to know who God is. Sometimes, circumstances in life which you think are your end are a tool for your victory and to help draw you closer to God. Never think of loss because of the poor situation you find yourself in. The condition is there for only a moment; it will not be there to the end of your lifespan.

Never be discouraged, because of the hardship you are going through. Exercise faith in God and be hopeful until the end. Hard times are opportunity days to discover your real being and your destiny. Never doubt God because of hard times. In life, hard times teach us lessons of bitterness and the carefulness we should know for our progress.

We must accept every condition we are in and manage it well. Never announce your condition or make the noise of your situation. All our conditions are aspects of our life's progress and benefits in every situation.

In this world, every life has its record and reward. The lives we live cannot be equal; so are the situations that we are passing through. Every life has its unique ways and conditions that one must pass through.

Never think that you are cursed because of the hardship you are going through. Sometimes, life becomes unbearable but do not think it is a curse. You may even prefer dying to live. That is, you dislike existence in its entirety. But never kill yourself; look up to God for a breakthrough, and good things will happen to you.

Bad days are like taking bitter drugs, but bitter drugs are remedies for some bad situations. It is evident that bad days also produce good results and bring out new ideas. '

All things work together for good to those who love God...' (Rom. 8:28). So never give up on bad days. God has thousands of ways to provide for you. Never be discouraged, for your possession is available to claim; take it.

55. Life's carefulness and profit

Life can be sweet by carefulness and determination. And proper attention is the key that reveals knowledge and understanding. Carefulness brings good wealth and gives profit even to the foolish. Having a fresh thing with a fresh mind is better than an old thing used by an unknown person. A new experience brings new knowledge; new knowledge brings research, and research brings broad knowledge and understanding. A fresh husband is better than an old husband who wants to become fresh. In life, some people want to get everything on a silver platter rather than use accepted laws and regulations. So many people take things for granted. Taking precautions prevents an accident, and .it helps to rightly do things. Some people don't think before they act; rather, they act before they think. Almost always, we make mistakes in the things we do. Sometimes, we do things hastily without considering what the outcome would be. We always pack up before thinking. But profit comes by the carefulness of doing things. Never fail to plan; if you do, you have planned to fail.

56. Today's women and fashion

I do not, sometimes, understand women in this world about how they want to appear. In fact, I can say women are the world. I ask myself what women want from this world.

This world is for women. What are the women searching for? What do they want to do? Human appearance makes him a real being. Women do not care for certain appearances concerning what they wear.

Our world today is moved by women. They do not care about what they wear, whether it is good or bad. Interestingly, they are moving this world into destruction by what they wear.

Some women of today are promoting fornication, because of what they wear. They appear to engage in provocative dances on the dancing floor.

Human beings are, sometimes, known by what they wear. Life in this world is short, and we do not know what is in store for us; that is, no one knows what will happen to him or her. This world is running out of time. We hear bad news every day. But many women of today do not care about anything concerning life.

The dressing has brought a lot of damage to the human mind, and this has blocked correct thinking, which can bring about wonderful things into our world.

Wearing of indecent clothes lures people, and it has caused a lot of accidents in our world. Women of the day have damaged this world with what they wear. I have a question for them. Who is a Christian? Does Christianity say anything about what women wear?

When you enter the house of God, the same dress which you will see in the world is what you find in the church of God.

Women of today have become promoters of fornication through what they wear. Woman, who is Christian? Woman, what do you want from the world which is passing away?

Today, you cannot differentiate between a Christian woman and a worldly woman. Women have become channels of evil because of their clothing since what you wear defines you. When you dress badly, you reveal bad character and the bad character reveals bad destiny. There is nothing that identifies a person's character more than the person's adornment. What you wear reveals your character and reflects your status in society.

Sometimes, people are known for their adornment. Many men have become fornicators because of what some women wear. Women of today have no excuse for what they wear, and they cannot say that worshipping God has nothing to do with how you dress. What you wear is a matter of concern for Christianity.

A Christian who is of good standing can fall because of a woman's indecent dressing. In fact, all dresses identify characters. Accordingly, I can say that an indecent dress is a tool for fornication.

Human beings have lost the covering of glory God endowed us with when the human race sinned and became naked. It was this merciful God who covered our nakedness with proper clothes. If you wear indecent clothes, you promote sin.

Most women promote adultery through their dressing. It is difficult to say something about the clothes women of today wear. This is because these clothes appear almost everywhere.

Many people wear the same clothes to church, parties, clubs, meetings and so on. Today's fashion has brought a lot to confuse other women who want to be modest. Consequently, such women are torn between what is decent and what is socially acceptable.

One trait of fashion which some women carelessly follow is wearing a pair of tight trousers that reveal their body contours. This type of clothes promotes fornication and adultery.

The world has become women, and women have become the world. Clothes are characters, and the fashion of the day has become a channel of destruction. Women must be careful.

'Moreover, the Lord said, because the daughters of Zion are haughty, and walk with stretched-forth necks and wanton eyes... making a tinkling with their feet...' (Is. 3:16-26).

All our adornments communicate with our followers and those around us. Wearing of clothes speaks a lot than the waves of the sea; it needs a great amount of carefulness.

The adornment of today's women has destroyed proper communication and has damaged the world's beauty.

The dressing of the day has put our world into a pit of sin, and this is a potential for man's doom. Many of the women of today have caused mind traffic and have damaged a lot of minds for correct thinking.

57. Making it fruitful

Gentle words are words of comfort. Words of comfort are words of encouragement. Beautiful words give advice and cheer. Every life is prospered by words of comfort and gentleness.

Words of encouragement promote life and make it fruitful. Our life progresses with the reception of good words. This makes life abound.

A lot has been said but little has been benefited. Too many words profit nothing but little words of comfort can move away mountains that block progress.

Your life needs to progress and improve with gentle words. Gentle words are sweeter than honey; they build one's courage. A word of hope builds old walls and establishes broken cities.

That is, those without hope can be established by gentle words whispered to them. Our lives sometimes need to hear words that are very gentle, before they can rise to their proper positions.

You can pursue your wishes but you may not progress without gentle words or words of encouragement. Your establishment needs words of encouragement. You can be whatever you want to be. However, without words of comfort, you cannot progress.

We must be careful about the kind of words we speak to others. As human beings we need words that will guide us to grow into our purpose; without words of encouragement, our lives will be in great danger.

In order to make it well, we need the word of God to properly survive. Without that, nobody can properly survive. So to make your life fruitful, you need Christ Jesus in every aspect of your life.

Many people want to succeed through their own effort. They are most likely to fail; no matter how hard they try, it will turn to nothing. It is not by might or strength or any knowledge; it is by His Spirit and help (Zechariah 4:6). This enables us to survive and be successful.

Many have failed because they depended on their own strength. Your fruitfulness depends on God only, not anything else. Never think you will force and become successful; you will fail totally.

Consider God in all the things you do and you will prosper. Seek the kingdom of God above all else... and he will give you everything you need (Matt.6:33).

58. Beautiful but fake appearance

It is not all that twinkles that is gold. Many people deceive others with their false appearance. People search for only the beautiful but what they search for are not beautiful enough.

We always hasten in choosing beautiful things but fail to think of their results. In life, we need to be careful about the beautiful things that we chose. Many people have made mistakes in their search for beautiful things.

Beautiful things are sometimes deceptive. Loving beautiful things become loving empty wells. In life, we need not think of beautiful things only; we need to consider the result or the outcome too.

Many fail to choose the right thing because they first consider beauty. We need not be absorbed by great things in life; rather, we need to consider what the outcome of the decision will be.

We always consider beauty other than its quality and fail to plan for the quality of beauty. We substitute love for moonlight instead of starlight but still want what is better than best. In life, what is great and good is sometimes considered little, but the unnecessary are considered much. We always love funny things than serious things and make a mockery of our salvation.

Never appreciate beauty without quality; rather, appreciate the quality in beauty. Do not just choose charming things; rather, choose quality things even if they are not highly regarded.

Beautiful things are heard of in many announcements but quality in beauty is veiled. A name is nothing without good behaviour. And a good name is identified by good behaviour.

Do not pursue beauty without quality or charm without quality. Be observant and always consider the outcome of your decisions. Not all things are good.

But we can find out what is valuable. Be considerate when making choices. May God guide you to select. Never rush when something charms you; be vigilant and think twice before you act. That will help you to live well in this world.

Looking at beautiful things involves a lot of things that can result in good or bad experiences. Everybody needs to have right thinking when looking at anything beautiful so that it does not end poorly. A poor result can be your doom forever.

Everyone needs to be careful about the things that are pleasing to their eyes. You shouldn't be deceived by beautiful things; rather, be careful when you are looking at them.

Worldly beauty calls for bad attention and it results in emptiness. But the beauty in Christ calls for abundance and ends in eternal life. Which beauty are you pursuing?

59. Marital Situations

Many marriages have missed their proper standings. Right partners have mixed up. Impatience in entering into marriage has brought a lot of mismatch in husband and wife.

So many mistakes have been made by different people as they enter into marriage. Uncontrolled lust has made many people choose the wrong partners, and the result has been detrimental to them. Some people have made mistakes in the choices because they considered only money.

People marry wrong partners because of appearance; others marry to avoid fornication but have failed. Still, others marry out of pity. Many marriages have missed their right partners because of some situations.

Some marriages have lost their sense of value because of the wrong choices of partner. Sometimes, both partners become accusers of each other; that is, they throw words at each other. Those who are ready for marriage must carefully wait upon the Lord for their right partners.

60. Life's waves

When life misses its rightful point, it behaves like the sea waves. When life is uncertain in all points, it moves in directions whose control is difficult.

Sometimes, life becomes like walking in a muddy area; you do not know where to step. You are, sometimes, confused about making decisions. It takes time for you to take a step in a muddy area. That's how life is. It takes patience to make a step forward.

Never let the life that seems like walking in the mud slow you down; move, never standstill. Make your direction anywhere you like and move ahead to get out from the mud you see.

Walking in the mud makes your movement slow; so is life. Life needs patience to move along. Life is not like walking on an asphalt road where you can run or walk faster as you wish.

Life can silence you, like a dead lake. The faster you want it, the worse it becomes; the brighter you want it, the darker it becomes; and the sweeter you want it, the bitter it becomes. But this is the qualification that life needs for its pure growth. Never think it will be easy for you to step forward in life. It needs patience and carefulness.

Many people want to get quick money and to enjoy luxurious cars and other pleasurable things. But what is the benefit of all these, if you do not have Christ?

Life requires awareness, determination, truthfulness, proper planning and the help of God for success. Never let your hardship block your progress or prevent you from planning.

Try to build your house, regardless of the season. That is, take advantage of every situation you find yourself in; never give up. Life is how you want it to be and the condition in which you want yourself.

You cannot control everything life brings your way but you can own a better life by your willingness and attitude. Life cannot be entirely controlled but it can be won by choice. A better life is no respecter of age; it is a wish. Life must not stand still; it needs to pursue a wish – the reward for that life's choice. Never think of the difficult circumstances you go through as misery or a barrier to your progress; rather, let them motivate you to press on.

Bad wishes lead to bad choices and bad choices also lead to bad conditions. The condition of your wish leads to an expected outcome. Plan to have a better condition so that it will lead you to a better destiny. Life consists of negative and positive branches and the fruit which it must bear to show the seed that was sown.

In life, the first seed one sows – whether good or bad – can be a mark that identifies the starting point of that life. A good foundation determines the strength of the whole building.

A life well established brings hope for the future. Every life starts with a struggle of a sort. Through that struggle, a choice is made which brings your destiny.

Never leave God behind; never build a life without Him. Never think that you can have a life of true peace by your effort. A sea wave brings out something; so does a life of progress.

Human nature changes during the process of growth. In life, a change of situation brings maturity or immaturity depending on the choice that is made. Every life needs to struggle. However, it must bear a fruit – or fruits – to reveal its identity.

What struggle are you going through? You need to notice every stage of your life because it is a lesson which will help you to change your way of living.

Human life starts in the womb of a mother. The keys that initiate that life into success depend on the mother's action towards the baby in the womb. Thus, the nature of a person's life depends partly on a mother's actions and inactions towards the baby during pregnancy.

Life's hardship mostly benefits us. But life's curses mostly depend on our mother's actions towards us. Mothers must, therefore, be careful about their actions towards their children.

Life is about actions and inactions. But life's prosperity stands on choices. Never be down-spirited because of hardship; be courageous and move forward. All people may be against you but you will be successful in the end. The waves of life are inevitable. Sometimes, life can seem hopeless and dark as if you will not be successful. But be hopeful and courageous; never let it go.

Have faith in God and hold on to the end. Things will be better and profitable. Let your desire to success guide you to press even harder, when things are tough. Discover what you need by searching deep.

Discuss, work it out and hold on to the end. Never abuse your dignity or throw out your inner beauty because of your hard situation. Let your hope be in God, and be of good courage.

61. Innocent but suffering

Because of sin, people have lost insight to differentiate between good and evil. Good judgment has lost the right position. The innocent suffer wrongful punishment and the guilty go without punishment.

Sin has blocked sound judgment and justice. Good people suffer for bad ones; others have been put into prisons without offence and have suffered unjustifiably.

Sometimes, poor persons suffer because of their poor state; they could even suffer for another person's mistake. In this world, wrongdoers enjoy themselves because they live by the principles of the world.

The world has changed due to the high level of sin, and sin is the ruler of everything. Wrongs have become right and rights have become wrong in the sight of the world.

Bribery has become the food of the day, and corruption has become the sunlight. World leaders use their powers to steal; they pride themselves in corrupt acts, make laws in their favour, create to steal, and deceive weak people. Some people who lack knowledge become sycophants of such leaders.

These leaders do all kinds of things and surround themselves with giant security persons. They feel no guilt when they inflict pains on people and abuse laws of the land.

The leaders of the world promote devious acts. Despite all these, they act as if they have the interest of the people at heart. Power corrupts them absolutely; they cheat the system with money.

The blameless suffer for not agreeing with the world's decisions; the leaders of the world promote wrong acts. Servants are the riders of the world but royals are suffering in life.

62. Only one out of a thousand

Life stands out for one particular thing – character. It is that which uniquely identifies a person. Our character singles out each person and makes him or her real human being.

Our life in this world thrives well on one thing – character. Our speeches walks, and actions make up our character. People know you by your character; they love you by your character, and others hate you by your character.

People appreciate you by your character, come to you by your character, avoid you by your character, welcome you by your character, and reject you by your character. The only home of yours that people can identify is your character.

Character consists of the kind of behaviour we exhibit. It can determine your destiny forever. We need to watch out on our attitudes and behaviour each day.

The time offered us by God needs careful consideration with our actions. The only fruit that God needs in his kingdom is our character. Good behaviour forms a good character which is a sign of good identity.

Our life's identity depends on the character. All is waste if we gather all things and fail to gather good character. It is unnecessary. You can become who you want to be. You can be a hero of all heroes, and you can be first in all things done on earth but your character must count more than all.

You cannot share your character but your character can let others know you. Never feign your appearance, because your character can reveal it to others.

You will lose your appearance when your real character comes out. Your name is your character and your character is your name. That is, your character will be your name in the coming days and that will determine where you should go.

What is your character? What character are you building? Some people's character identifies their face. Some strive for worldly properties but not a good character.

Our character will be our name in heaven. The only property that heaven needs is our character. God will not accept anything short of Him. Why do people worry themselves over things that profit nothing?

A good name is better than riches. That is, a good character is better than great wealth. Where are you focusing your life? Let me assure you that this world is not your home.

What is your decision? Where are you heading towards? What will be your next place of abode? Which destiny do you want? Your character today will choose your home tomorrow. Watch out!

63. Poor situations

God created every human being for a particular purpose. Accordingly, every person has a unique way of living God's glory. But sin has changed the situation of our living.

In life, everyone must have what is necessary concerning the situation in which the person wants to be. God created us one but different in standards and capabilities. We were not created to be poor. In fact, sin has blocked a lot of chances that God gave to man, and this has devalued our standards.

Life needs proper ingredients to function well, and every human must have needs suited for his or her standard. We are not created to be equal but to have relatively equal needs.

A poor situation can block valuable potentials. Poverty can lock out the mind of creativity and great achievements.

Poverty is the wall that blocks hope but a poor condition is like swimming undersea waves. Human beings are created to help each other, and everyone needs help to survive. Life needs assistance to progress and to achieve something. Everything is for all people, not you only. Never wait for help; be ready to help others, and help will come to you unawares. Be nice to everyone who you come into contact with.

Help the needy, if you can; wish them well. Always let your words be a blessing to others; you will be a real blessing to all. Be kind and smile to everyone you meet. By so doing, you will be a relief to others.

Without a poor condition, the life of everyone will lack blessing. This is so because blessings come by giving to the needy. If everyone needed nothing, then to whom would you give what you have? Where will the blessing through giving stand? Giving will not be necessary.

The poor situation of someone is the key that opens a door for another's blessing.It is God who created life from the void. This shows that without God there would be no life in this world. Every life needs help, for it betters a situation. Never avoid someone who needs your help; it may lead you into a curse forever. Always be ready to help others, especially the needy.

64. A Journey without rest

This world is not our home to stay in forever. We must carefully consider our lives each moment and watch out wherever we are heading towards.

There is no rest or vacation in the journey of this. The journey we have taken upon ourselves is eternal. Meanwhile, enemies are always on the move to prevent us from reaching where we are supposed to be.

'God has planted eternity in the human heart; but even so, people cannot see the whole scope of God's work from the beginning to the end' (Eccl. 3:11). The way is so long, and it takes our whole lives to reach.

It involves tragedies, diverse circumstances, sorrows, trials, etc. These are snares to discourage us and test our temper with the sole of preventing us from going forward to achieve our goals. These ceaseless grumbles go on every day.

We have no rest or relaxation moment in life, for the devil is always ready to attack and take us captive. A person's life is always at risk; there is no second chance when we lose it. We need not complain. You need to be focused to resist the attempts to take you captive.

The most dangerous thing in this journey is to respond to the circumstances by resting or by being indifferent. There is no rest in this life. Life needs constant communication with God. Human beings need to have faith in God, to overcome trials and attacks of the devil.

Let me address men at this stage. We need to monitor our everyday life and to watch out on every step we take each moment. So many people have been taken captive by the devil, because of certain circumstances.

Never be worried about your trials; consider the outcome and stay alert. Be ready to brace the trials but never go with it or entertain it. Do not rest, until you reach home; rest not, till you receive the crown.

Our life in this world is always a war, and there is no rest. A journey without rest is also a ceaseless activity, which involves all the necessary tools for its completion. All human beings need to think beyond what we see and imagine.

This earth is not our home; we have eternity before us, and we need to work day and night, to attain the enviable crown God has prepared for us. Let all people be considerate and determined not to lose the precious eternal city. Let us stretch forth our hands to receive it. Amen!

For Good Living and Knowledge Gain!
B. B. S. LIFE BOOKS.
The Science of Life

Also by Bernard Benson Sarfo

The Fact Among Facts (1st)
The Fact Among Facts

Standalone
The Youth Murderer
Be Original Not a Copy
The Christians Science or Scholarship
Precious than Paradise
Habit makes future
A shelter from storm and rain
The Science of Life
The Strongest Lion Knockback
The Perfect and Inspiring City

About the Author

Bernard Benson Sarfo is an acquainted architectural designer and a motivational speaker.He is a gifted teacher who continues to motivate and encourage many.

Read more at https://www.amazon.com//author/bbslifebooks.